MY KINGDOM FOR A LAB!

MY KINGDOM FOR A LAB!

Life with the Hunting Labrador Retriever

E. Donnall Thomas Jr.

WILLOW CREEK PRESS

Published by Willow Creek Press,
P.O. Box 147, Minocqua, Wisconsin 54548

Design: Amy Kolberg

Library of Congress Cataloging-in-Publication Data

Thomas, E. Donnall.
  My kingdom for a lab! : life with the hunting Labrador retriever/E. Donnall Thomas, Jr.
      p. cm.
  ISBN 1-59543-245-0 (hardcover : alk. paper)
1.   Labrador retriever. 2.   Hunting dogs.   I.   Title.
  SF429.L3T483 2005
  636.752'7--dc22

                                                                 2005016327

Printed in the United States of America

Table of Contents

Acknowledgements

In different form, much of this text has appeared before in magazines including *Ducks Unlimited, Just Labs, Traveling Wingshooter, Big Sky Journal, Alaska* and especially *Retriever Journal.* I appreciate the opportunity to rework the material for inclusion in this volume.

I would like to express my gratitude to Steve Smith, Jake Smith and Bob Butz. In their various editorial capacities with *Retriever Journal* and its sister publications, all three allowed me tremendous latitude to test the limits of the envelope and write about the world of hunting dogs as I saw fit. Without their support, this book would not have been possible.

Dedication

To the loyal patients in my medical practice, who never complained when I made rounds in muddy boots and tolerated my absences during hunting season even when I found ways to stretch it out to twelve months a year.

You have made my other profession a privilege and a pleasure.

Introduction

Countless books have been written about retrievers, a number of them excellent. The most widely read concentrate on telling readers how to train and manage their dogs, worthy subjects to be sure. For several reasons, not least of which that I would not presume any ability to add to this body of knowledge, this collection of stories and essays will be different.

A friend once wrote an article exploring the division of outdoorsmen into specialists and generalists and I think he had a point. The net sum of knowledge possessed by members of each group doesn't really differ, but in the specialist's case experience and the wisdom it begets lie concentrated in a narrow area of expertise: hunting turkeys, catching trout on dry flies, or training retrievers to win field trials. Readers seeking to expand their own command of any such subject should generally look for books written by specialists.

Alas, I may be the quintessential generalist simply because I enjoy so many elements of the outdoor experience and pursue them with more or less equal degrees of passion, activities that include bow hunting, fly-fishing, wingshooting, dogs, outdoor photography and wilderness travel. Because I've devoted my entire life to these interests—and, to the best of my ability, few others including work—and because I almost never depend upon the services of guides and outfitters, I've learned a considerable amount about all of them. But I don't know enough about any of these fields to match the accumulated wisdom of the true specialist, and I refuse to pretend differently in print.

Readers who just need to know how to begin training their first retriever should consult one of the many excellent instructional texts devoted to this subject. That's not to say the astute reader won't be able to learn anything in the pages that follow, particularly concerning topics such as upland hunting in the American west, wing-shooting opportunities in Alaska, and the remarkable versatility of the Labrador retriever. But, with respect for the old precept of prose composition, expect to be shown rather than told and be advised that we'll spend a lot more time exploring why you should enjoy the company of a retriever than how to train one.

In fact, this real subject of this book isn't retrievers per se, but the nature of the relationship that develops between hunters and their dogs over the course of long hours together under circumstances ranging from familiar to challenging. And in that aspect of the Labrador retriever's world, I may actually qualify for specialist credentials after all.

UPLAND GAME

U pland bird hunting may seem an odd topic to explore at the beginning of a book about Labrador retrievers. Amphibious athletes born and bred to thrive in the aquatic environment, Labs practically define American waterfowling and many of their traditional enthusiasts regard as heretical the idea of them doing anything else. But as we shall see, no dog defies its own stereotypes as eagerly as the Lab.

Given their dominating credentials in the waterfowling world, Labs would seem to typify the concept of a specialized sporting breed. But the dogs, as usual, have other ideas. Turns out Labs take readily to the pursuit of just about anything worth shooting with a shotgun, and the limited, waterfowl-specific job description they enjoyed for years owes less to any limitation on their part than to lack of imagination on our own.

Over the last three decades, I've enjoyed the company of Labrador retrievers while hunting just about every species of upland game bird found in North America (and a number on other continents as well). The rugged hills and coulees surrounding my Montana home provide ample opportunity to appreciate a Lab's upland talents, but I've also hunted with my dogs in venues as diverse as Alaska's frozen tundra and the arid desert southwest. While no upland bird demonstrates the value of a flushing retriever quite like the wild ringneck, I've used my Labs productively on species as diverse as ptarmigan, chukar and quail. In the process of acquiring all this personal experience in the field, I've learned an important lesson about my dogs: if it has feathers and I'm interested in hunting it, they probably will be too.

Much as I enjoy the company of Labs, I'd never pretend they make an optimal choice in the pursuit of all these upland game bird species. Only a highly insensitive hunter could fail to appreciate both the beauty and the practicality of good pointers working ruffed grouse or quail. But here in the West, a hard day of hunting may involve everything from Huns to geese, and no breed I know rises to so many occasions as well as the Lab.

So come on along as we revisit some of those experiences, and be prepared to keep an open mind about the breed's original job description in the field.

Opening Day

The ultimate celebration for hunters and dogs alike

W hile sagebrush bathed in sunlight projects a truly unique color, it doesn't look purple at all. But I suppose Zane Grey couldn't have written a book called *Riders of the Silvery-Green Sage* unless he wanted to return full time to the practice of dentistry, which should tell us something about the perfidy of writers whose imagination sometimes exceeds their grasp of the subject. Now thousands of acres of the stuff rolled away ahead us beneath the early light, empty and featureless as the sea. A heavy dew fall overnight had filled the air with the pungent scent of moist sagebrush and the invigorating, faintly alien smell poured through the truck's open windows as we bounced along from one corner of Nowhere to the next. The impression of splendid desolation practically took my breath away, for we were new to the country then and utterly captivated by the excitement of opening day on the prairie.

My old friend Dick LeBlond rode beside me in the truck's front seat. Burned out after a grueling year of medical internship back east, we had followed my father's advice and volunteered for a two-year Indian Health Service stint in the isolated northeastern corner of Montana. The draft was over then and the IHS—a branch of the uniformed services—was having trouble filling assignments in remote locations. When Montana IHS recruiters heard that two qualified physicians actually wanted to go to the

Fort Peck Reservation, they greeted our interest with near disbelief. While Dick and I were young and strongly motivated by
social conscience, the tales my father told of the fabulous bird
hunting in those parts certainly helped make our decision easier.
Sometimes action based on principle earns its own rewards.

Behind us in the bed of the truck, Bogey, my young yellow
Lab, thrust his eager muzzle into the torrent of smells sweeping
past as we drove. I'd been able to work him some on ducks the
previous year, but internships are rarely compatible with serious
hunting and he had never enjoyed any opportunity to hunt
upland game. In all honesty, as newcomers to those glorious
wide-open spaces, Dick and I didn't know a lot more about
prairie habitat and the birds it contained than the dog did.

As shooting light finally broke over the eastern horizon, we
crested a low rise and broke out above a creek bed that contained
a smattering of cottonwoods to disrupt the sage's apparent
monotony. The creek bed seemed as good a place as any to start.

By serendipity we had stumbled
upon an important principle: in
dry prairie habitat, low-lying terrain collects the moisture that
produces the cover that concentrates the birds. Nonetheless, we
still felt like sailors leaving port
as we loaded our guns, released
the dog, and set off into the
Great Perhaps.

I can't pretend to have felt any
great measure of confidence in
Bogey. My skepticism proved well

founded, as he eventually matured into one of the most intractable Labs I've ever known. But three hundred yards into the cover, I rounded a bush and stumbled upon a truly amazing sight: Bogey locked solidly on point. I'd never heard of a pointing Lab and back then I'm not sure anyone else had either, but after a childhood squandered in New England grouse cover I sure knew a point when I saw one. I called to Dick but before I could begin to explain this unlikely situation the still morning air began to yield to the sound of straining wings.

No amount of experience could have prepared me for that first encounter with sage grouse. The birds' sheer bulk suggested a dance choreographed for quail but performed by wild turkeys and as they clamored their way into the sky I managed nothing more effectual than an open-mouthed stare. Part of the problem was scientific; back then, I needed a moment of deliberation to distinguish between dull-colored sage grouse, sharptails, and illegal hen pheasants, a process that now takes place subconsciously in milliseconds. But it was the spectacle itself that undid me. The birds simply looked too big to believe.

Fortunately, early season sage hens in remote locations have never been known for their guile. As Bogey abandoned his previously unappreciated pointing instincts and began to nose through the cover, more birds erupted in stately, measured rises not even a novice could flub. "Sage hens!" I finally managed to blurt out, and then Dick and I fell to the task of isolating targets from the confusion. At close range, the slow-flying birds offered easy shooting and despite our rustiness we quickly sent several crashing to the ground in a series of immensely satisfying whomps.

That morning, Bogey's disappointments still lay safely shrouded in the future and he collected the downed birds in workmanlike fashion. We didn't even bother to mark the escaping flock, for our first encounter with sage hens in the hand felt like a special moment and we were smart enough to pause and savor it. When we finally collected ourselves, reloaded, and set off down the creek bottom, the brace of birds in the game vest felt like a hindquarter of venison dragging at my shoulders and the cover ahead looked endless and vaguely foreboding. Not that we cared; our legs were young, the dog was eager, and the whole season lay spread out before us.

Even after five decades in the outdoors, I've never lost my appreciation for the special phenomenon of opening day. While intended to ensure wise management of wildlife resources, legal seasons actually serve a higher purpose: the periodic elevation of the outdoorsman's mood to an uncontainable level of excitement. Back when I was a little kid, the madness began on April 1, the opening day of trout season, and repeated itself three months later when bass season began. Once I grew old enough to hunt, the anticipation of opening days reached new levels of frenzy characterized by sleepless nights, exhaustive strategy sessions, and compulsive fiddling with guns and gear. Nowadays the calendar includes all manner of opening days as my interests have broadened: turkeys in April; grouse, partridge and doves on the first of September followed by archery elk, deer and antelope; bears a week after that; waterfowl in early October; pheasants a week later; and finally mountain lions in December. That list doesn't even include fishing or seasons in other states. A life that rich in opening days can't be all bad, and believe me, it isn't.

Somehow it's still that September bird opener that evokes the best of the old anticipation. Despite occasionally great local fishing, August passes lazily here on the high plains, and with all due respect to the angler's craft few trout arouse the passion of fast game birds anymore, at least for me. The opening day of bird season marks an abrupt transition between summer languor and autumn madness, the period of aroused instincts and sleep deprivation during which nothing but the unfortunate demands of work can keep people like me out of the field. I find myself longing for it months in advance. How many months? Oh, nine, or thereabouts… the anticipation usually begins on the last day of the previous season.

I've often wondered if the dogs feel the tug of opening day too. While it's difficult to credit even the keenest canine brain with an ability to read the calendar, I'm convinced they feel anticipation on some level, at least after a few seasons of experience. Things just start getting a bit nuttier than usual around the kennel during the last week of August. Tails wag harder and the barks that greet each opening of the back door sound a little more inspired. By the night before the event itself, the dogs begin to act like kids on Christmas Eve, especially when guns come out of the cabinet and game vests appear draped over the backs of kitchen chairs. Dismiss this behavior as a simple learned response if you will, but they sure seem to have trouble containing their enthusiasm.

No wonder. I know just how they feel.

A nother piece of prairie, another September… The truck rattles to a stop on a windswept knoll overlooking a long series of coulees winding away toward the north. The mid-morning sun has set the hoppers buzzing through the grass as the temperature climbs leisurely through the comfort range. While

some opening days obligate serious hunters to rise in the dark, this isn't one of them. In fact, prairie grouse hunting often improves later in the morning as birds gather in thicker cover close to the shade. At least this observation provides a convenient rationalization for the extra hour of sleep we enjoyed this morning, even if it does sound suspiciously like an excuse.

As young Jake explodes from the confinement of the truck, Sonny shows his age by stepping gingerly down to ground level like an uncertain swimmer testing the shallow end of the pool. His days of starting the first day of bird season by trying to run in four directions at once passed years ago. Now he's content to leave those antics to Jake. I can still tell that he knows what's up, but he confines his demonstration of enthusiasm to tail wagging and flapping his ears, a wonderful economy of motion that convinces me he's saving himself for more important things to come. It occurs to me that this display of wisdom should probably not be lost upon his human companions.

The plan is to work both dogs down through the scattered brush along the bottom of the nearest coulee and return through the grass and wild roses along the side hill. If we don't have a limit of sharptails by then, we'll leave Sonny at the truck and hunt Jake on through the heat of the day. Without thinking, I lower my voice discreetly as I explain this plan to Lori. With nearly a dozen opening days under his belt, Sonny deserves to begin this one without hurt feelings. Silly sentiment? Well, sure… but anyone who has hunted an old campaigner into the twilight of his years ought to understand.

As much as I appreciate enthusiasm in flushing retrievers, there is also a time for restraint, and as I chamber a pair of shells, I whistle Jake to my side. No sight sinks the spirits like clouds of birds exploding before an uncontrolled dog. Canine eagerness becomes futile in the absence of discipline, and this is my opening day too.

A hundred yards down the draw, we reach a promising clump of buffalo berry and I urge Jake toward the brush. Betraying the inexperience of youth, he begins to hunt intently through the grass behind us, the one place I feel confident the birds are not. Suddenly old Sonny picks up his head and plunges—as best a dog his age can plunge—into the guts of the cover. His sudden focus can only mean one thing. "Here they come!" I shout across the coulee at Lori, and sure enough. Heard well before they're seen, a pair of sharptails fights its way upward through the foliage and suddenly clears the leafy branches right in front of us: the first glorious rise of the year.

No bird on the wing invites a shotgun's swing quite like a sharptail. With two birds down quickly and the retrieves neatly divided between the dogs, a sudden sense of déjà vu transports me back to that first prairie opener years ago. Despite the similarity of impressions, it's hard to ignore all that has changed since then. Dick has left Montana to become a respected professor of medicine at a large university. Bogey is long gone, replaced by a succession of dogs ranging in ability from modest to great. I have no photographic record from those early days other than a few faded snapshots, which is probably just as well. The trim waistline and absence of gray in the beard seem startling when I stare back across the years at the kid I used to be.

But somehow the important things remain, and that's what really matters in the end. As much as the hunters may have changed, good country, good dogs, and good friends somehow manage to endure.

And it's still opening day.

Society and Solitude

Alone, but never lonely

October's cool nights have left Montana's creek bottoms awash in color, golds and crimsons that will stand until some final combination of wind and snow conspires to overwhelm them with winter's unforgiving chill. The hour-long trip north from the house provides a visual feast for the eye that anticipation only serves to intensify. Serving as unofficial tour guide, I point out areas of historic interest as we drive. This narrative comes heavily flavored by personal experience and local knowledge, with terrain features identified by the shooting that once took place near them. My visitors absorb this chatter with interest that goes well beyond politeness, and the fascination on their faces reminds Lori and me at once what a wonderful world we inhabit and how much we sometimes take it all for granted.

But my pickup is a hunting vehicle and not a tour bus, and however well intended, talk can only sustain us so long. When we finally pull off the county road, cross a cattle guard, and pull up at the edge of the pheasant cover, I still feel the same old pee-in-your-pants excitement I remember from bird hunts forty years past, in no small part because of our visitors' contagious enthusiasm. The frantic chorus from the dog box only adds to the general excitement. This morning I have brought along Sonny, the old veteran, Jake, the rising star (we hope) and Kodi, an English setter too young to know anything but too much fun to leave behind.

Although they have every right to feel fatigued after a day of airports and a night of food and stories at our house, Dick and Marshall climb down out of the rig wearing looks appropriate to kids leaving school on the first day of summer vacation. We don our vests, check our guns, and study the cover. There are decisions to be made about the dogs. Because it is early in the season and we all really want to shoot some birds, we elect to leave Kodi in the truck, over Lori's modest protest. But I've learned over the years that you shouldn't hunt young dogs when birds themselves are the first order of business, an explanation that Lori somewhat reluctantly accepts. Finally, it's time to go hunting.

The cover here consists of a thick, nasty tangle of willows laced with beaver stobs winding its way between two stubble fields and none of us pretends it's going to be easy. I volunteer to take the dogs through the guts of the cover while Dick and Marshall work the edges and Lori follows with the camera. Within moments, we're all out of sight of one another. Such situations make me edgy when I'm hunting with people I don't know well, but I've shared enough cover with Dick and Marshall to know I don't have to worry about their gun handling. All my attention belongs to the dogs and the task of negotiating my way through the willows.

I crash and I crunch, and finally find an open seam along the old creek bed where I can move in relative freedom. Even so, it's obvious I'm not going to do a whole lot of shooting down in this stuff. Suddenly, that no longer matters. Somewhere up ahead, one of the dogs noses a bird into the air and a loud cackle identifies it as a rooster. Someone shoots, extinguishing the racket. As I climb up onto the bank and into an open glade, another bird rises. "Hen!" someone cries alertly above the noise. The sound of more wings follows, and then another shot, and it finally starts to feel like pheasant season.

Lost in the fog of war, I'm busy trying to locate Sonny and

Jake. Suddenly I hear an inarticulate cry of delight from Lori and both dogs appear, each with a rooster in his mouth, seeking me out in tandem as if it never occurred to them that anyone else could have shot so surely. And the sight of them is beautiful to behold: two Labs, one young and one old, framed by the morning sunlight, doing what they have been raised to do and what they know best. This is no time to dispel illusions. With silent apologies to my companions, I accept the birds as if I'd killed them myself and then it's time to move on, back into the cover to make it happen all over again.

These are my friends and my dogs. Despite the inhospitable cover and the silent shotgun in my hand, I wouldn't have it any other way.

At our house, October is the social season for a variety of reasons. For family and friends, it never hurts to enjoy a standing invitation to the heart of good bird country. And for my own part, I'm always ready for some genuine camaraderie by the time pheasant season rolls around, especially after six weeks of intensive bowhunting, which must rank as one of the most solitary undertakings in outdoor sport. And it doesn't hurt that autumn is one of the most pleasant times to show the high plains off to visitors, give or take an occasional early blizzard. Seeing your own backyard through the eyes of guests can alert anyone, anywhere to subtle pleasures of home that might have been overlooked without the benefit of company.

As hunters become progressively isolated from a society that no longer seems to understand our passions, it can be difficult to realize how much the hunt has contributed to our own species' social integration. Study the Paleolithic cave paintings of Spain and southern France. Hunting was something we did when we did practically nothing else together. As an enthusiastic if informal student of human affairs, I can't help but think that matters as diverse as parliamentary government and the origins of speech itself derive directly from the need to communicate effectively in order to get game in the bag at the end of the day. Granted, my opinions may suffer from certain biases, but still.

At our house, the grand tradition of hunting with others as a means of social expression reaches a climax during pheasant season. That's when my parents love me the most, and who can blame them? Friends I haven't seen in years drop in out of the blue, and that's fine with me too. After hours, our kitchen becomes the epicenter of all this good will, and it's hard to imagine a social obligation more rewarding than the preparation of wild birds for those whose company I genuinely enjoy. If there are flaws in my schedule at this time of year, they only have to do with the occasional need to sleep and work, facts of life to be dealt with like sticky ejectors or hard-mouthed dogs.

And I'm convinced the dogs themselves get into the spirit of the social season. Many of our visitors want to bring their own dogs along and I'm all for it; when you're trying to boot wild ringnecks up out of the brambles, the more dogs the merrier. And at the end of the day when we've all gathered around the stove to solve the problems of the world, there's no reason not to have a passel of pleasantly exhausted canines underfoot. In fact, it just wouldn't be the same without them. Should they grow unruly, we can always banish them to the kennel. If only we could do the same with the kids.

But for all the pleasures that company can bring during hunting season, there must also be a time to leave the hurly-burly behind and experience the natural world without distraction. I usually reach that point sometime in November, although my sudden withdrawal from company then should never be construed as rejection of the good times that preceded it. But just as the presence of others whose judgment you know and trust can enhance the appreciation of the natural world, so can its absence, a realization that implies the need to hunt alone from time to time.

Alone… except for the dogs, of course.

During the final week of one recent bird season, I took an afternoon off from work and drove thirty miles from town to a remote ranch owned by a family I've known forever, the way you can only know people forever when you live out in the middle of the prairie. No one was around, but it didn't matter. I knew where I was going and my invitation to hunt the place has stood for years.

After a two-gate drive down a twisting dirt track, I stopped the truck at the edge of a field and climbed into the pure winter air. A hundred yards away, I could see a dozen spots clustered in the golden wash of stubble, as anomalous as measles on a baby's cheek. Soon a head went up and then the pheasants flushed, sailing across the field toward a little finger of buck brush that led downhill to a coulee that led farther downhill to another coulee in endless permutations of terrain. These were cagey late season ringnecks and I suspected Sonny and I might never see any of them again, but that didn't mean we couldn't try.

There was no snow on the ground, and the country seemed to be having trouble deciding whether to dress for fall or winter. At the edge of the field, the grass lay listlessly underfoot and the brush had Cassius' lean and hungry look as it ran away into the yawning breaks ahead. Walking reluctantly at heel, Sonny made it plain that he didn't care about the scenery. All he wanted was a chance to find some birds, and when I clucked him ahead he attacked the cover as if it were hiding someone who had insulted his family honor.

The pheasants from the stubble field had vanished like ghosts and we didn't fly a bird until we turned into another of the main coulee's many tributaries. Suddenly Sonny was making game and then the bird was right in my face, so close I had to make myself hesitate before shooting to keep from blowing dinner to pieces. It was a beginner's straight-away to tell the truth, but it didn't matter. The bird was dead, the dog was happy, and so was I.

It took another hour of up and down to flush two more roosters and then we were done. Because I had been following the cover I wanted to hunt rather than a route that would lead us in a logical circle back to our starting point, we were a good two miles from the truck when the dog delivered the third and final pheasant. With the afternoon sun behind us, we began the long uphill pull back toward home.

As I finally crested the rise above the far end of the field, a ripple of noise began to sweep through the leftover grain and then the air was full of wings. The birds were sharptails, gathered into a vast flock of hundreds. Bunched-up late season sharptails seldom allow an approach within shotgun range, and the dog and I just stood and watched as they all flushed wild into the still winter air. I hadn't seen that many sharptails together for years. The shotgun felt superfluous; it was enough to look and listen, and to let the great chattering cloud of birds remind me all over again what I love about living on the prairie.

Back at the truck, I took off my shooting vest, cased the gun, and let Sonny ride up front with me. I'd spent the whole afternoon detached from the busyness of the modern world, without speaking a word other than the easy *Heel-Fetch-Good Boy* patter of dog talk. In many ways, the solitude felt as welcome as the limit of roosters, but I still felt an odd, undefined tug of longing for human companionship, and as I started down the long road home, I finally recognized its origins.

I needed someone riding in the shotgun seat to climb out and get those damned gates.

Despite my enthusiasm for company at certain times of the year, I've never objected to hunting alone. Sure, some of my solo ventures take place because Lori and the kids and my handful of regular hunting partners are all busy doing something else. But then there are days when I don't spend a lot of time looking for them, either.

That's because enjoying the outdoors is one of those spiritual exercises that often fails to reach its fullest expression in the company of others. No matter how welcome it may be at times, companionship in the field implies responsibility. For safety's sake, you need to keep track of your hunting partners' whereabouts. Even though that process becomes nearly subliminal with experience, it remains a subtle distraction. And you also need to worry—at least a little bit—about whether your companions are having as much fun out there as you. There's certainly a time and place for such courtesy, since consideration lies at the very heart of friendship itself. But it's also important to respect your own need to hunt alone from time to time, and to take the measures necessary to satisfy it.

Despite the strategic advantage hunting partners can sometimes provide in the field, I often have an easier time shooting limits of birds when I'm by myself. I usually do better addressing the cover on my own terms, at my own pace, with dogs capable of reading my intentions as surely as I can read theirs. But hunting solo really isn't about bag limits. No matter how much you enjoy their company, other hunters invite distraction rather than intensity, chatter rather than the appreciation of its absence. There is a time and place for both the social and the solitary view of the natural world, but it seems to be the latter we most consistently neglect.

Of course, good friends are priceless, and no one appreciates that fact more than a seasoned outdoorsman. Shoot an elk deep in some hopeless blowdown, watch a good dog break through the ice, or roll an airplane into a ball on a remote gravel bar, and you'll learn all about the value of friendship in a hurry. (As you might guess, I've done all three, and I still enjoy hunting with the friends who helped bail me out of those various predicaments.) But there remains a time to leave all that behind and take what nature serves you straight up.

Fortunately, the absence of other human companions does not necessarily mean loneliness. When it comes to the primal need to be reminded that one is not alone in the woods (never mind the universe), it's hard to beat a Labrador retriever. Dogs assure us that wingshooting never needs to be a lonely undertaking. Sure, dogs can't talk, but that also means that they can't argue. (Some learn to express their disdain for bad shooting, but they're usually easy enough to ignore.) And how many of our best friends have never done anything worse than hard-mouth a bird or shake water around a duck blind? I rest my case.

The best hunting dogs enjoy a remarkable ability to accompany you without getting in your face, a social skill many of our two-legged friends could benefit from learning. So let us agree to leave the dogs off the list of companions we should forsake from time to time as we head for the field. In contrast to people, Labs seldom distract from the occasional need for an undiluted dose of the wingshooting experience, and there is no reason to turn your back on company like that.

Alone without feeling lonely… leave it to the Labrador retriever to master that remarkable slight of hand.

From Veldt to Tundra
The far ranging world of Labs afield

Insects buzzed noisily through the dull curtain of heat as raptors turned lazy circles overhead. Green hills studded the horizon, but the grassy plains in front of us lay parched to a golden brown as the countryside waited patiently for the first welcome rain of the season. Dogs began to stir beneath the tarp covering the back of the truck as we rattled to a stop, climbed out and began to ready our gear. Just another eagerly awaited day of bird hunting, and for a moment we might have imagined ourselves back on the Montana prairie.

In fact, we were about as far from home as it is physically possible to get, and the illusion of commonplace circumstances proved fragile immediately. The first cue came from the sound of the birds in the trees overhead. Instead of the subtle chatter of meadowlarks, the incessant three-note dirge of Cape turtledoves greeted our ears: *work-HARD-er! work-HARD-er!* Then a gentle patter of Shona rose behind the truck as our old friend Will Schultz discussed strategy with Isaac and Juoa, the two dog handlers. A wart hog's sudden explosion from the dry grass completed the transformation from the familiar to the exotic. As I watched the boar scamper across the field with his tail held high, I knew: like Dorothy in the Land of Oz, we weren't in Kansas anymore.

According to the wisdom of another generation of old safari

hands, once you've visited Africa you'll always long to return. I
might have served as a poster child for this obsession. Ever since
my first trip to Africa a dozen years earlier, I've schemed constantly to return and my nearly annual ability to do so has proved
a remarkable testament to my disregard for everyday considerations such as day jobs and financial responsibility. At least Lori's
enthusiasm for the place spared me any marital discord as a con-
sequence. Now we were back in northern Zimbabwe, visiting
places and friends we hadn't seen in several years, and not even
the political turmoil wracking this once lovely country could
deter the enthusiasm of our return.

As a former British colony, Zimbabwean culture still reflects
strong measures of imperial influence, ranging from official use of
the Queen's English to a stubborn insistence upon driving down
the wrong side of the road. In the case of the cuisine, such colo-
nial influences may be better honored in the breech than the

observance, but not when it comes to the appreciation of wing-shooting traditions. As we released the dogs and loaded our guns, I found myself grinning in anticipation. Zimbabwe might have its troubles, but our friends there still knew how to hunt birds right.

Organized at last, we set off through the cover with our Alaskan friends Joe Sangster and Alex Russell on one flank, Lori and me on the other, and Will and the two handlers holding the center behind a brace of splendid English pointers. I've always enjoyed watching pointing dogs work, as a matter of fascination rather than intimacy. While I like to think I understand Labs, pointers and their behavior always seem amazing, and hunting with them leaves me vaguely confused, like listening to music sung in a foreign language. Despite the graceful way Will's dogs covered the ground, it didn't take my attention long to shift from the stars out front to a far less flashy member of the canine team: Storm, Will's aging black Labrador.

While as personable as any worthy representative of the breed, Storm seemed perfectly content to concede the limelight to the pointers. Reflecting her training in the British tradition of the no-slip retriever, she might have passed as Will's shadow. She never required a verbal reminder to keep her in her place, which appeared to be exactly two feet behind Will's left ankle. Trying to imagine how one of my own dogs would have accepted this subdued role simply illustrated the difference between the classical retriever's job description and the one that has evolved in the helter-skelter pheasant-strewn world of the American West.

After a leisurely fifteen-minute hike across the grass, Rigby, the older of the two pointers, locked up so quickly I thought he might fall over and Sam, his partner, moved in quickly to honor. The covey of francolin held as Joe and Alex moved up behind the dogs and suddenly the air seemed full of wings. Joe dropped a bird that tried to squirt out behind him while Alex completed a snappy right-left double. By the time both shooters finished reloading frantically and the last of the stragglers took to the air, another pair of birds had fallen and it was time for Storm to go to work.

With the exception of the ringneck pheasant, nothing illustrates the utility of a trained retriever in upland cover like true covey birds: Huns, quail and, in this case, francolin. Fast shooting in multiple directions makes it difficult to mark fallen birds accurately, and whatever spatial memory you manage to create will likely be erased by a few subsequent rises. True to form, by the time the shooting stopped none of us could remember what had fallen where... except Storm. Despite rapidly deteriorating scenting conditions, she scooped up one bird after another and delivered each in perfect condition to Juoa's outstretched hand. Showing no apparent effect from the rising heat, she promptly retired to Will's side and waited for the hunt to resume.

By the time the heat forced us to retire from the field midmorning, we'd located another half dozen coveys, missed a few birds and killed a whole lot more. Thanks to Storm's workmanlike performance, every bird we dropped wound up in the ice chest back at the truck, bound for the kitchen. Hunting in rotated braces, the pointers had all performed splendidly under challenging conditions, but I maintained my own notions about the identity of the morning's true canine hero.

Of course, I've always been a Lab kind of guy.

Geographic distribution provides a functional definition of any domestic animal's usefulness and adaptability. Most breeds developed to meet needs specific to their point of origin, and relatively few demonstrate the two characteristics necessary to insure widespread dispersal courtesy of human travelers: universal utility to people and the ability to thrive under a wide variety of habitat conditions. *Sus scrofa,* the familiar domestic swine, represents a fine example of these principles. Derived from stocks of Old World wild boar, pigs became a widely popular food source among Eurasian peoples. Because they traveled well and thrived wherever they wound up, they accompanied both Polynesian voyagers and European sailors on the long voyages that resulted in the dispersion of both civilizations. Today, feral hogs prosper just about everywhere except the extreme arctic.

While one hesitates to compare Labrador retrievers to pigs, Labs, for similar reasons, may have become the world's most widely distributed dog breed. In the course of my travels, I've encountered them throughout the New World, southern Africa and the Pacific rim, where they seem to have found ways to hunt just about anything that can be pursued reasonably with a shotgun. Despite their origins as water dogs in the north Atlantic, they perform remarkably well in hot, dry habitat, as I've discovered all the way from the African veldt to our own desert southwest. And when they're not busy hunting, Labs have always found means to endear themselves to human companions of various cultural backgrounds. Even if they didn't enjoy such remarkable utility in the field, their enduring loyalty and enthusiasm would have made them perennial winners in the Miss Congeniality category. Perhaps someday I'll discover an outdoor venue that wouldn't benefit from the company of a hard-working Lab.

But it hasn't happened yet.

So much sunlight, so little heat… the essential paradox of a bright February day in the Alaska interior. The silence that rises to greet us as the Cub's skis chatter to a stop feels greater than any human artifice in the world. Stretching away uninterrupted in all directions, the frozen tundra might prove as liberating as Huck Finn's river or as foreboding as Ahab's ocean by the time the timid sun disappears once more. It's best not to think about the night I'll have to spend alone beneath the northern lights if the engine balks when I return.

In fact, I'm not really alone, not with Sky bouncing around beside me, thankful for his freedom after the confinement of the two-hour ride from home. As always, the ability of one yellow dog to make the wilderness feel a little less intimidating leaves me faintly amazed. At its best, canine companionship outdoors provides most of the benefits the human kind provides without nearly as many complications, a quality I've always found nearly as valuable as my dogs' ability to locate and recover game birds.

Because of our remote circumstances, the Cub requires a few extra minutes of care before we set off down the creek bed toward the ptarmigan tracks I spotted earlier from the air. With engine cover and tie-downs secure, it's time for one last executive decision before departing. I hate shooting birds while wearing snowshoes, which always seem to leave my feet planted in impossible positions when it comes time to swing and fire. But a long winter's worth of wind loading and freeze-thaw cycles have left the deep snow set up hard as concrete. Acknowledging that I may be pushing my luck, I leave the shoes behind, chamber two shells, and head for the nearby line of willows.

Hunting winter ptarmigan can be an unpredictable affair. Sometimes the white birds will hunker down in the snow and hold like early season sharptails (to which they're closely related), offering the kind of shooting that can quickly leave a hunter groaning beneath the weight of a legal twenty-bird limit. But they're just as likely to explode at impossible distances, chattering their way off across miles of frozen terrain never to be seen again. Today's first encounter suggests the possibility of a serious game bird dinner back home. As Sky hits the skids and dives into a clump of snow laden brush, a handful of ptarmigan erupts and offers an easy double, leaving me to admire the impossible whiteness of their plumage when the dog delivers them to hand.

But these birds prove the exception rather than the rule. The second flock flushes wild, offering nothing but the sound of their rich, reedy cries and the sight of their pearly outlines set against the distant azure sky. So does the third. But I manage to mark these birds down on a side hill a half-mile away, an observation that nearly proves my undoing. Thanks to its southern exposure, the snow there has collected enough warmth from the sun to turn sugary and rotten, and half way to the birds I've broken through the crust and bogged down to my axles. Prudence, a valuable personality trait in such circumstances, has never been my strong suit. Irrationally convinced the footing will improve just ahead, I flounder along nearly to the point of exhaustion. Supporting 80 pounds on four legs instead of 200 on two, Sky stays comfortably on top, bewildered by my predicament but unable to offer anything more than sympathy. On the old television show, this would be the point at which Lassie shows sense enough to Go Get Help, not that any happens to be available to us today.

Conceding defeat at last, I reverse course and flounder back to solid footing in the creek bottom. The first ten steps I manage without breaking through the crust feel like some kind of miracle. An hour later, we reach the airplane and the snowshoes I should have had sense enough to strap to my pack frame in the first place. The engine's quick growl in response to the starter button never sounded more reassuring. Then with Sky perched cheerfully in the rear seat, we're headed home at last.

Despite the ache in my thighs, the cold layer of sweat congealing beneath my woolens and the meager bag, it's hard to dismiss the day as a failure. We came and we saw, and even if we didn't quite conquer, we left with an enhanced appreciation of the wild world that still awaits us.

It's there, all right. Just ask the nearest Lab.

Feathers and Ice

The demanding world of late season sharptails

December marks the start of the lonely season here on the high plains, a time of inhospitable winds, lowering skies and vast landscapes painted in monochromatic shades of gray. Days usually seem ready to end before they've had a chance to begin and all too often the feeble sun can barely generate a shadow. Even heavily clad hunters find themselves walking relentlessly just to keep warm and there are days when no amount of wool and exercise can ward off the chill. All in all, the calendar's last page reads like a convincing argument for staying indoors, and it would be save for two considerations: the birds and the yearning we feel for them once the end of the season starts to stare us in the face at last.

Despite the competing allure of ducks and pheasants during the late season, I always try to find a little time for sharptails at this time of year. Somehow, they capture the spirit of the season's end better than any other game bird I know. The ringnecks hail from Asia and the mallards from Canada but sharptails remain true native sons, genuine products of the local prairie that somehow deserve an extra measure of respect for their trouble. In contrast to the waterfowl, they mean to stay no matter how tough the winter gets and since I'm in pretty much the same position it's easy to feel the same kind of affinity for them that people develop when they face difficult circumstances together.

And the dogs feel it too. As much as they enjoy waterfowl, my Labs are upland game enthusiasts at heart and they need a break from the relative constraints of the duck blind from time to time. And after weeks of progressively wilier roosters they seem to appreciate a break from pheasants too. Sharptails inhabit open country big enough to let the dogs roam and to offer a relatively favorable ratio of birds smelled to birds shot and ultimately retrieved. Sometimes.

Sometimes; ay, there's the rub. Wingshooters familiar with sharptails only in their cooperative early season form will need to alter both their tactics and their expectations before taking to the field at the end of the season. In contrast to pheasants, which concentrate in well-defined terrain that invites sustained hunting pressure, the changes in sharptail behavior that take place between the first week of season and the last reflect biology rather than education by dogs and gunfire. In September, sharp-tails remain organized in small family groups and the combination of thick grass and their superb natural camouflage encourages them to hold before they flush. By December, the grass is gone and snow cover renders their camouflage largely ineffective. Vulnerable to predators of all descriptions, they gather in progressively larger flocks and rely for security on their ability to see rather than their ability to hide. Early season sharp-tails may remind visiting hunters of quail, but by December the same birds are more apt to act like wild turkeys.

Years ago when I was still a newcomer to the prairie, I was driving back from a late season duck hunt when I spotted a large flock of sharptails feeding along the edge of a stubble field beside a narrow, brushy coulee. Assuming the birds would bleed down into the cover and hold, I parked over the nearest hill, let Sky out of the back of the truck, and set off to add a few quick grouse to the limit of mallards we'd already collected. Foolish me.

As soon as I crested the rise with my gun cradled in my arms and Sky obediently at heel, grouse began to flush wildly from the stubble field—not just the birds I'd seen earlier but dozens more, dozens that eventually swelled to hundreds. The air lay crisp and still that morning and the racket all those chuckling grouse made as they took to the air sounded loud as a jet taking off. It wasn't a matter of passing up shots at marginal range—the nearest birds were flushing over a hundred yards away. The dog obviously shared my frustration and I could tell by the eager whining at my side how badly he wanted to break and give chase, but he was old enough by then to make discipline in the face of torment a matter of pride. And so, deprived of immediate options, the two of us stood and enjoyed the show while I tried to dream up a way to convert all those birds into a modest grouse dinner.

As it turns out, our sharptail hunt had ended before it ever began, although neither of us knew enough to realize it. My Plan A called for marking the birds and walking them up when they finally settled back to earth, hopefully in thicker cover. But when they crested the nearest horizon three miles away they were still going strong, crossing more prairie with their characteristic flap-and-glide wing beat pattern than we could have covered in hours even if we had been able to see where they landed. Plan B—a superior tactic, as subsequent decades of sharptail hunting have taught me—consisted of working the nearest coulee for stragglers and we did, to no avail. Bottom line: we'd watched over 300 sharptails rise from one field without firing a shot, and finally returned to the vehicle with nothing to show for our effort but a little hard-earned wisdom.

From this experience and many others like it I derived my First Law of Late Season Sharptails: If you can see grouse on the ground, you probably aren't going to shoot them. Birds know when they're vulnerable, and if you can see them, they can see you. Visible birds seem to understand that since they can't escape by hiding, they are going to have to flush, the sooner the better. And since I've observed this behavior countless times in remote areas where birds haven't heard a shotgun all season, I'm convinced it represents a natural response to predation by foxes, coyotes, and raptors rather than human hunting pressure.

This observation raises an obvious question. Other than companionship and an occasional retrieve, what role does a Lab play in the pursuit of birds apparently determined to flush out of range in the first place? As it turns out, the answer holds the key to success at this quirky game.

Please excuse an illustrative digression. Years ago I made a pioneering trip to Christmas Island, now a standard stop on the saltwater fly rod circuit but then a largely unknown destination. Driving down the road the first morning, I immediately spotted—from the car, no less—large schools of bonefish sulking around in a lagoon, and I wasted a whole day trying to catch them before I realized those fish weren't feeding and had no intention of doing so. As soon as I made myself ignore them and set off to find less obvious but more cooperative fish, I caught bones by the score. The moral holds for all outdoor endeavors. If the quarry staring you in the face isn't doing what you need it to do, find one that is.

This principle certainly applies to late season sharptails. The sight of a large flock feeding across a snow-covered field may quicken the pulse but it's unlikely to produce a grouse dinner.

But when they're not feeding, grouse need to rest in sheltered areas out of the reach of hawks. With the grass beaten down, late season birds tend to take cover in the thickest brush around, usually silver buffalo berry, where they'll sometimes hold nicely even late in the year. And since sharptails don't run like pheasants, all you have to do is find them... as long as you're hunting with a dog willing to hit the brush. Needless to say, this job calls for a close-ranging dog. While I encourage my dogs to cover a lot of ground early in the year, by late season I usually work them from heel. By then, sharptails are only likely to give you one chance and the first rise better take place within shotgun range.

Now a brief culinary note... Young sharptails are one of my favorite game birds on the table and I prefer to prepare them simply, to take advantage of their tenderness and unique flavor. Late in the season however, sharptails become substantially darker and tougher, changes that no doubt contribute to their marginal reputation as table fare. While there's nothing wrong with them, late season birds will benefit from a little more preparation. Rather than roasting whole plucked birds as I do earlier in the year, I usually skin them, cut the meat in strips and marinate it prior to cooking. After going through all it sometimes takes to kill them, it's worth investing a little extra effort in the finished product.

Afternoons like this remind me why I left Alaska, for the thought of a darker, colder world seems more than the human spirit should be asked to bear. Far away to the south, the winter sun looks like a caricature of its former self, generating light without heat, a fluorescent rather than an incandescent light bulb. Crisp enough to demand respect, the air acts like an amplifier, not that there's all that much to hear: the chink of brass on steel as the shells drop into the shotgun's chambers, the crunch of paws on frozen snow as Sonny noodles his way around an abandoned piece of farm machinery searching for the perfect place to pee. But despite the chill and the loneliness this empty reach of snow and brush suggests, there's a haunting beauty to the landscape ahead. Despite? Let's make that because of. We all find reasons to inhabit the places we call home and solitude is one of mine.

While some hunts entail a certain amount of pomp and circumstance, this one is more of a quick hit: an early escape from town, a short drive into the country, no company other than the dog and no ambitions beyond a little exercise justified by the shotgun in my hands. Turning fifty has already taught me I'd better use it or lose it, but I'd rather use it outdoors than inside on a treadmill. Besides, Sonny's showing his age even more than me, and no one I know has figured out how to put a Labrador

retriever on a Stairmaster. Because of time constraints, we haven't made it to one of my slam-dunk pieces of sharptail cover, but this one will do. There are birds out there somewhere, and even though we may not find them before the end of shooting light, the possibility should sustain us until sundown.

Chores completed, Sonny makes a bold feint across the open stubble field beside the truck, but I really think the sound of my whistle arouses more relief than resentment. He'd like to tear off cross-country the way he used to when he was younger; hell, so would I. But we're both veterans now, with enough seasons under the belt to make us realize the value of patience in the pursuit of late season grouse. The long look on his face is just for show, especially once he's figured out that *heel* means I'm the one breaking trail through the snow, all of which reminds me that human beings are the only creatures on earth that actually have to seek out ways to burn calories.

According to convention, wingshooting stories should be full of, well… wings and shooting. Sometimes they are, but not tonight. For nearly an hour, it's just me and the old dog and the country and that's enough. Our strategy remains simple. Eschewing the swales and coulees that might have held birds two months earlier, we plod from one tangle of buffalo berry to the next. Each time we reach one, I position myself as strategically as possible and send in the dog. At every stop, Sonny snorts and snuffles his way through the thorns at his own geriatric pace, but I'm not worried. Canine noses age more gracefully than canine legs, and if we can find cover with birds in it I feel confident he'll accomplish his end of the job.

But tonight the cover seems determined to send me home a hiker rather than a shooter. We've crossed from the head of one long draw to the next and started back toward the truck when a sudden chatter of wings catches me flat-footed with the shotgun draped haphazardly over my shoulder. By the time I have the index bird picked out against the sunset, it's nearly out of range and I hold my fire in deference to the Second Law of Late Season Sharptails: Where there's one, there's more.

Indeed. Thank God; the thought of old Sonny going to all that effort just to watch me stare passively at the only rise of the day would almost be enough to ruin an otherwise delightful afternoon. But in typical December sharptail fashion, the problem of not enough birds has yielded to the problem of too many. Picking two targets from the sudden crescendo of wings careening away in all directions proves to be the only hard part of the shooting, and just like that it's over: two birds dead in the snow, two dozen more sailing off into the sunset, and everything the dog and I could have asked for a matter of record.

Even now, I can't imagine a better way to end a season.

Water Dogs in the Desert

*Labs are never out of their element as
long as there's something to hunt*

The escarpment of weathered rock rose from the desert floor
like an act of geological defiance. Early morning light
glowed back at us from the mantle of prickly pear sprawled
across its flanks and for a moment it was possible to forget just
how hot it would be in another hour. I had run into the quail the
day before while bowhunting javelina. Covey after covey had
erupted from the sparse cover along the base of the butte but
there was nothing I could do then but watch them fly and track
them with an imaginary double.

Now my bow lay back in the truck and I had everything I had
longed for earlier: my parents, both of whom still hunt birds
enthusiastically, my shotgun and my dog. Enough sneaking
through the cactus worrying about the wind and searching for
elusive desert pigs... we were all going bird hunting, and not a
moment too soon for my taste.

Sonny certainly seemed to agree. He had hunted the previous
day with my folks and served them well according to their
account, but he spent the evening offering the plaintive looks he
always gives me when I leave him behind during bow season.
This morning, when he saw me slip into my game vest and
slide the shotgun from its case, he burst into celebration,
bouncing around the truck in a mindless display of canine

enthusiasm. Save it for later, I wanted to tell him. You're going
to need it.

We finally set out toward the base of the butte with my
mother on one side and my father on the other while I brought
up the middle with the dog. The Arizona desert always looks
like rough going at first, but much of its terrain provides surprisingly comfortable walking despite those first impressions, with
hard but reliable footing and plenty of room between all those
thorns. The rising sun behind us made the desert glow with color
and the landscape offered so many distractions as we walked
along that I almost forgot to pay attention to the dog.

Sonny, I have to admit, would have had trouble passing
muster as anyone's idea of a classic quail dog, especially in country that didn't hold enough water to make mud. Our party might
have looked more conventional hunting behind Brittanies or set-
ters, but Sonny was the dog we had. Besides, I have yet to find a
game bird whose pursuit doesn't benefit from the presence of an
enthusiastic Labrador retriever.

My attention lost upon the desert flora, I was busy consider-
ing the various ways each variety of cactus had adapted to its
habitat when I caught a glimpse of Sonny with his nose to the
ground. As I shouted a warning to my folks, a covey of Gamble's
quail erupted in a buzzing rise that reminded me of a swarm of
bees. Unaccustomed to the birds' tiny size, I stood and stared
until a straggler rose and crossed in front of me near the edge of
shotgun range. I could plainly see the bird's topknot, which
meant I was staring at the quail rather than swinging the gun.
That's why I missed with the first barrel, but then I settled down
and watched the bird fold with my second shot, leaving a delicate
puff of feathers suspended in the still morning air.

Argue all you will about what kind of dog does the best job before the shot; when birds are down, I'll take a Lab no matter what the circumstances. I marked the fallen quail in a dense cluster of prickly pear and by the time I reloaded Sonny was in the thick of it, avoiding thorns by some remarkable process of instinct. Somehow, he burrowed his way through the stuff unscathed and emerged from the other side with the quail in his mouth. All three of us felt sure we never would have recovered the bird without him, at least not without paying a terrible price courtesy of the thorns.

After the initial rise, the covey settled into a jumble of talus at the base of the butte. We regrouped and worked our way toward the birds with Sonny at heel. We walked right into the middle of the area where I had marked the covey, but the desert remained silent until I released the dog.

Moments later, he nosed the first bird into the air right in front of my father who dropped it easily. Then a second bird flushed underfoot. I marveled at its speed and delicate size until it was safely in the clear and then I swung and slapped the trigger and watched the perfect vector of the bird's flight disintegrate as it folded. We stopped to let the dog retrieve the two downed birds but he couldn't get the job done without running into more quail. For several minutes matters became very confusing, and when the shooting finally stopped we broke our guns and stood and watched the dog work until he had collected what had fallen.

As we circled back along the base of the butte toward the truck, we jumped a second covey and my father made a snappy double that left me hoping I would be shooting with the same authority when I'm his age. I scrambled across the rocks to help the dog with the retrieves but Sonny already had the second bird

in his mouth by the time I reached my father. "Look at this!" he said as he held the two birds out for inspection. He had taken a true mixed double, a Gamble's and a scaled quail. The scalie looked stunning and exotic with its jay-like crest and neck hackles that reminded me of classic Atlantic salmon flies. We stood and admired the brace of birds until the dog reminded us quail season hadn't closed yet, and then we spread out and began to search for the scattered covey.

We had the whole day ahead of us, but patience never means much to a Lab with the smell of game in his nose.

Coming from Montana, I should be casual about the pleasures of western scenery, but there's still a breathtaking quality to the splendor of our great southwestern desert. Visual artists from Ansel Adams to Georgia O'Keefe made careers celebrating the enchanting quality of its light. Furthermore, the Arizona desert remains beautiful and accommodating even in the middle of winter, when the mountains and plains back home have grown cold and dark and outdoor recreational opportunities have dwindled to acquired tastes such as lion hunting, coyote calling, and ice fishing. Arizona's quail season runs through mid-February, and with generous limits, ample public hunting ground, and three species of birds—Gamble's, scalies, and the strikingly plumaged little Mearn's—even the most ambitious wingshooter should have trouble running out of things to do there.

Using flushing retrievers to hunt desert quail may sound unconventional at best, but a seasoned Lab can make a major contribution to this exciting game. Locating birds dispersed in wide terrain always goes better with canine legs and noses on your team. Initial covey rises often take place at marginal range even in front of pointing dogs and I'm willing to concede those rises without much shooting, especially since desert quail seldom fly far and are usually easy to mark down after that initial flush.

Few jobs in the field invite a pointing dog's skills quite like working broken coveys of quail. That doesn't mean a good flushing retriever can't be useful in the same situation, provided the dog remains under control and has a good nose. Offering explosive rises and tricky shot angles, tightly holding quail can provide exciting wing-shooting, but hunters will walk right by most such birds without a trained dog to aid in their location. Labs may lack the elegance of the pointing breeds, but they'll always find a way to get the job done.

Assuming you've located a covey, broken the birds up and managed to shoot a few, you'll eventually appreciate the services of retrievers doing what retrievers do best. Even in open terrain, dead quail look an awful lot like the desert, and with birds busting from the cactus in all directions, most of us have difficulty marking falls. With an experienced retriever along, there's no reason to take your eyes off birds still in the air.

Working retrievers in desert terrain requires handlers to pay special attention to their dogs' physical needs. The retrieving breeds are bred to stay warm in cold weather, not the other way around. The same physiologic adaptations that allow them to work comfortably in frigid water also make it easy for them to overheat after long miles beneath a hot sun. Dehydration and heat stroke are serious veterinary problems that can fell even a fit, healthy dog in less time than it takes to tell.

Carry plenty of water in your vehicle and offer it to the dogs frequently. Rest them at regular intervals, ideally by using more than one dog in rotation. During rest periods, be sure the dog has access to shade, which can be hard to find in the middle of treeless desert terrain. Above all, never leave a dog inside an enclosed vehicle, where the temperature may rise quickly to dangerous levels on a sunny day. When working dogs in rotation, leave those at rest kenneled outside in the shade of the vehicle.

Cactus thorns are generally not as hazardous to dogs as they might seem, although cholla can cause problems in areas where it grows heavily. I'm not much of a believer in dog boots although others swear by them. Fortunately, sand-burrs—the best argument I know for canine footwear—aren't common in most of the areas I've hunted Arizona quail. (South Texas quail cover is another matter.) Duct tape wrapped around dogs' feet makes an excellent substitute for boots should you encounter difficult conditions, and the stuff is so useful a roll belongs in every hunting vehicle anyway.

The most important principle in the prevention of all these problems is the recognition that you must do the thinking for

the dog, whether the issue is
heat, rest, water, or thorns underfoot. That's because the dog will
be too busy hunting.

Late afternoon shadows are
reaching out from the base
of the hills as the desert sunlight
begins to soften at last. I arrive
back at the rig dead tired, not so
much because of the miles I've
walked but because of the miles
I've glassed, studying the desert
for signs of the elusive javelina.

My folks are somewhere up the draw hunting with our friend
Rich Johnson and his dog. They are well out of sight but I can
mark their progress with my ears by the sound of the shooting.
Sonny lies curled up in his kennel beside the truck, enjoying a
well-earned rest. But as I sink to one knee and look inside, he
fixes me with the doleful stare of the abandoned. And I thought
I'd been doing him a favor.

Vaguely ashamed, I unstring the bow and reach inside the rig
for my vest and shotgun and by the time the kennel door opens,
Sonny and I are friends again. A little draw lies just up the road
and the absence of boot prints in the sand suggests the rest of
our party hasn't hunted it yet. There isn't much to the draw, but
at the end of a long day like this, there doesn't have to be.

We work our way along for twenty minutes without flushing
a bird. Across the valley behind me, I spot three orange vests
heading toward the truck as I cross the wash and turn around to

do the same. In country as big as this, there always comes a time to put the guns away, pluck some birds and enjoy a cold beer, and now that happy moment is bearing down on all of us like a collision.

But Sonny has other things in mind. As soon as we cross the draw and start up the other side, he snaps into focus. Suddenly a small covey rises in a riot of noise leaving me to pick a target out of the confusion. When one bird tumbles followed by another, the double seems like such a perfect way to end the day that I don't even bother to reload.

At least that's what I tell myself when the dog completes the second retrieve, and that pleasant fiction will sustain me on the walk back to the truck even though I'm really just too damn tired to chase the covey. Sonny is too, although he's even less likely to admit as much. One way or another, the desert has helped us come to terms at last; an old young man and a young old dog headed home together to await the arrival of another day.

WATERFOWL

Golden expanses of prairie marshland crackling with life beneath an Indian summer sun. Remote North Pacific beaches, lashed by wind and tide. Delicate spring creeks steaming beneath a frigid prairie sunrise. All familiar venues to the experienced waterfowl enthusiast... and the Labrador retriever.

As much as I've enjoyed the upland rambling I've done with my dogs—and the opportunity it's provided to celebrate the Lab's versatility—hunting with a Lab over water always feels like an overdue homecoming. It's in the blood I guess, mine and the dogs' alike. As much as I loved hunting grouse and woodcock when I was a kid growing up in upstate New York, nothing I did outdoors could rival the sheer spectacle of duck hunting. Even at an early age, I often preferred sitting in a blind all morning to following the pointers through the upland cover around our home. Centuries earlier, the Lab's ancestors swam the seas off the Newfoundland coast, retrieving nets, lines, buoys and fish for their masters. When it comes to water, neither the dogs nor I have ever looked back.

Physically, Labs always seem happiest while swimming, and no wonder. Water is the element to which they're born and bred. The Lab's tail—the same awkward instrument that scatters delicate objects from shelves and coffee tables around the house—serves the dog splendidly as both propeller and rudder the moment it leaves dry land. The same coat that covers the furniture with shed hair represents a triumph of marine engineering: sleek and streamlined, an efficient insulator even when wet, capable of drying in a shake—literally. Perhaps it's easier to understand Labs if you think of them as marine mammals, like otters or seals. I've certainly never met one that didn't take to the water immediately, even as young pup.

We've seen what they can do in settings where hunters could once scarcely imagine them. Now let's accompany them to the places they love best.

Moving Water

Retrievers in fast current demand a new set of rules

By the end of last duck season, young Rocky was hunting with poise beyond his years—all one and a half of them. In addition to demonstrating companionable blind manners and a splendid mouth, he'd started to show real maturity as he scanned the skies patiently for incoming birds and hit the water with confidence. Thanks to a long stretch of warm weather, we'd done most of our late season duck hunting over open sloughs, but on the final day of the season I decided he was ready to graduate to the kind of hunting that ordinarily defines December waterfowling here on the high plains. It was time to introduce him to the creek.

Under ordinary winter weather conditions, which include plenty of sub-zero cold, the spring-fed stream that runs through the valley we call home provides the only open water around. Ducks flock to it and mastering the current's tumbling flow remains a benchmark challenge for all our retrievers. Rocky had spent plenty of time on the creek over the course of the summer, training and tagging along while I stalked the banks with my fly rod, but he had yet to face the confusion of downed mallards bobbing away in its grip. The creek remained an important step in his education and I couldn't think of a good reason to delay his introduction to its challenges any longer.

As we left the house in the dark to drive to a friend's nearby ranch, I couldn't shake the feeling that I'd forgotten something

critical. We'd reached the first gate by the time I realized I'd left
my shell vest hanging back in the garage. This blunder took
nearly an hour of prime shooting time to correct. When we
finally arrived at the pool where I planned to set up, an eruption
of greenheads reminded me immediately how much being late
can cost a duck hunter. Trying not to think about all the mallards
we'd missed at first light, I set out a dozen decoys, settled into
the brush with the dog at my side, and began to wait.

Another hour passed before I enjoyed an opportunity for
redemption. When the flock of twenty banked and set their
wings, I rose and dropped a drake across the creek with my first
barrel. It took a moment to isolate another drake from the flaring
flock, and when I slapped the trigger again a second greenhead
tumbled into the riffle below the pool and set off downstream
with a broken wing.

I lined Rocky up on the more difficult retrieve, but, in typical
young dog fashion, he remained fixated upon the dead bird in
plain sight and I couldn't whistle him off the obvious fall.
Thanks to the brisk current, the cripple was already too far
downstream to anchor with another shot. By the time the dog
delivered the first bird, the second was already out of sight
around the next bend. After running the banks to no avail, we
returned to the decoys with at least one of us in a dejected
mood. I hate losing downed birds with a passion, and the realization that we'd done so because of a mistake any young dog
could have made—not to mention a less than perfect shot on
my part—provided little solace.

Perhaps our proud team wasn't ready for the creek after all.

I've always been surprised by the lack of attention the retriever
literature pays to the problems of working dogs in moving

water. Granted, personal circumstances have given me more experience than most with the subject, but I can't be the only duck hunter who shoots birds regularly on creeks and rivers. Trouble is, current produces counter-intuitive retrieving situations for dogs bred and trained to mark and hunt the area of the fall. I've seen fine, experienced dogs reduced to utter frustration the first time they work moving water simply because the current has removed the bird from the location they marked. While training dogs to cope effectively with this situation involves occasional elements of heresy, the results will prove worthwhile to those who value recovered birds more than adherence to conventional definitions of style.

Most water dogs will adjust to swimming in strong current fairly quickly, but it still pays to introduce them to moving water under controlled conditions, during the summer, with no birds at stake. They'll need to learn how to compensate for flow as they swim and how to pick routes up and down high banks, knowledge best acquired under friendly conditions. For those of us who spend a lot of time on trout streams, this kind of experience comes as a matter of routine canine companionship during the off-season. Others should make a point to work their dogs in current before hunting season if they plan to hunt ducks in similar conditions during the fall.

My hunting partners and I begin to introduce our dogs to the concept of *downstream* at an early age. Once the dog has mastered basic yard work, sit him on the bank, drop a dummy in plain sight, and let it drift off a way before sending him on the retrieve. Progressively extend the length of the drift. This teaches the dog to track a target on the water and introduces an important concept: the dummy may not be waiting in the same place it fell. On narrow streams, switch banks periodically so the dog learns that the bumper is moving downstream, not simply from left to right (or vice versa). On winding creeks, gradually let the dummy drift all the way around the next bend and out of sight before sending the dog. Under actual hunting conditions, he may lose track of the bird, but at least he'll know which way to look.

No situation in the field makes it more important that the handler be able to control the order in which the dog tackles multiple retrieves. Shooting over decoys on a creek often leaves a bird or two dead in plain sight while another floats away on the current. The easy birds can wait. Of course, controlled doubles are a part of basic training, but I still try to enforce the important points in the creek before the season. Drop one dummy in an obvious, stationary location such as a bank or sandbar. Then throw a second into the current. Progressively increase the interval between the second throw and the time you send the dog after it, giving the dummy time to drift away. This will make the visible dummy a more appealing target, but correct the dog as needed whenever he heads in the wrong direction. This lesson will teach the dog to ignore the obvious fall and go where you've told him, even when the object of the retrieve has drifted out of sight.

Which brings us to the subject of running banks, one of those heresies referenced earlier. I know what dogs are supposed to do in order to win field trials, but I also know what they have to do in order to avoid losing ducks on streams under hunting conditions. If that means taking short cuts, I'm all for it... as long as the dog remains under control and purposeful. With experience, several of my better Labs became absolute masters of cutting across current and running banks in the pursuit of drifting ducks. Their ability to calculate the angles reminds me of a defensive back cutting off a receiver after a catch in the secondary. This is

one of those issues that should remind us that we all have different goals for our retrievers. Purists forgive me; mine is losing as
few ducks as possible each season, and if that means allowing my
dogs some stylistic latitude, so be it.

No discussion of this subject would be complete without
addressing the most important issue of all: canine safety. As
noted, current itself rarely poses a problem for water dogs, and an
experienced retriever should be able to work comfortably—and
safely—in any open water likely to attract ducks. Obstructions
are another matter. As any canoeist or river rat knows—and I
qualify on both counts—sweepers on outside bends can overwhelm anyone or anything pushed against their upstream side. In
modest current, dogs can learn to negotiate most such obstacles,
and I give mine plenty of practice under controlled conditions
that don't represent a threat to their safety: in shallow water, during the summer, with me by their side. And I always adhere to a
simple rule of thumb. I don't work my dogs upstream from any
bank obstruction I couldn't easily escape from myself.

Ice shelves are another matter. Any retrieve made upstream
from ice covering running water deep enough to swallow a dog
represents a prescription for disaster. And when that disaster
strikes, it will do so with such shocking speed you likely won't be
able to do anything about it. Remember that an eager dog pursuing a wounded duck can cover a lot of water downstream in a
hurry. In cold weather, I always scout my hunting locations in
advance and avoid areas upstream from ice shelves. While I've
never had a serious mishap with one of my own dogs, a good
friend lost a promising Chessie under river ice many years ago,
and he nearly suffered the same fate when he tried to rescue the
dog from a hopeless situation. That sad experience made a last-

ing impression on all of us. Consistently erring on the side of
caution, we've declined a lot of promising shooting opportunities
in icy rivers since then. But without regrets… no limit of ducks
justifies sending a dog into current above an ice shelf.

B ack beside our decoy spread, I'm fretting away the morning
for reasons that have nothing to do with the empty skies
overhead. Despite Rocky's inexperience, we've hunted for a
month without losing a duck, and I hate the thought of retiring
for the winter on a sour note. The bird we lost has become more
meaningful than the rest of the limit I could probably shoot if I
stayed. Shouldering the shotgun, I heel the dog and we set off
downstream together in search of what really matters.

And nearly a mile below our decoy spread, damned if we don't
find it. I will never cease to be amazed by how much water a
determined mallard with a broken wing can cover. But as
Muhammad Ali once warned some hapless opponent: you can
run, but you can't hide… at least not from the Greatest, or a
Lab's nose. When Rocky flushes the bird from the grass along
the bank, dog and duck hit the creek in a geyser of spray, but this
time there are no fatal distractions. For a moment, young Rocky
looks like an old pro as he swims the mallard down in the chop,
reminding me briefly of Sky and Sonny in their prime. Sure,
we've got some work ahead of us before the next season begins,
but suddenly I can feel the potential in the air, the uncompromising determination to complete the retrieve that comes from
within the best of dogs and nowhere else.

Beneath the Northern Lights

The unique flavor of Alaska waterfowling

No stranger to the air, Sky leaned into the turn right along with me as I banked over the tide flats. From his resting spot high on the Cub's rear seat, he placed his nose against the window and studied the potholes for ducks as the edge of Cook Inlet slid by beneath the wing. I hoped he liked what we saw better than I did. While a few small flocks lay scattered about the polka dot patches of water below, the big push of birds from the northern interior had yet to arrive. But this was the last week of September in south-central Alaska, the time of year when anything could happen, and since I didn't need much from the day except a duck dinner and some quiet, I set up to land on the little patch of grass that passed for an airstrip beside our cabin.

The quiet came easily enough. In fact, you've never really heard the sound of silence until you've shut down an aircraft engine and stepped out into the delicious loneliness of the Alaska bush. That morning, not even the frolicking dog could extinguish it. After tying down the airplane and digging the shotgun out of the storage compartment behind the back seat, I walked up to the cabin for a bag of decoys and then Sky and I set off across the marsh.

Already beaten down by several weeks of intermittent frost, the grass felt like a rough, wet mattress beneath my feet. But I'd have traded better footing for the visibility any day. Brown bears prowled the flats on a regular basis, and if there was one around,

I didn't want any surprises. We jumped a green-wing off the first little pothole we passed, but I didn't bother dropping the decoy bag to shoot. All week long decoying birds had haunted my dreams—feet extended, wings set—and I just wasn't ready to start jump-shooting teal. Not yet.

On a crisp, clear day, the tide flats on the west side of Cook Inlet can be as visually spectacular as any waterfowling venue I know, with snow-capped volcanic peaks towering on one side and the angry sea churning along the other. But that day a layer of dull gray scud lay just high enough overhead to allow the flight from home in the first place. No matter; I could see everything I needed to in order to hunt, and I could imagine the rest.

For two hours after I set the decoys out in a little pond that looked no better and no worse than all the rest, those gray skies remained stubbornly empty. Finally a single teal appeared—for all I knew, the same bird we'd flushed on the way in—and my cramped legs straightened awkwardly as I rose and fired. The chip-shot retrieve allowed Sky a splendid opportunity to anoint

himself in tenacious black mud, a bounty he generously shared
once he returned to our makeshift blind. Those who would scoff
if I told them I didn't care must not realize what welcome company a muddy dog can provide in a remote wilderness setting.

Suddenly Sky, whose ears were better than mine, stared
upward. Following his gaze, I saw what he had heard: the season's first really large flock of mallards descending in wild vortices hundreds of birds thick. When the first fragment of the
whole set their wings over the decoys I stood and shot. Before I
could reload, another set came barreling in over the dead grass
only to flare in Sky's face as he tried to concentrate on the first
retrieve. I managed to snap the double closed and drop another
bird from the flock as they climbed back into the sky and then I
sat back to watch the dog work and enjoy the show.

No place I've ever hunted rolls the dice as quickly or enthusiastically as Alaska. One can only hope those dice aren't loaded.

Long famous as a destination for anglers and big game
hunters, Alaska also offers spectacular wingshooting opportunities, especially for ducks and geese. But like everything else
about the Great Land, Alaska waterfowling offers challenges
above and beyond the wildest corners of the Lower Forty-Eight.
Newcomers who fail to respect the unique outdoor demands of
the far north will eventually find themselves uncomfortable and
frustrated... assuming they survive.

Start with the weather. Cold isn't the issue; by the time the
thermometer plummets seriously, the ducks are usually gone anyway. I've endured far colder temperatures hunting waterfowl on
the plains of Montana. Wind and rain are another matter, for
such conditions can produce hypothermia even at moderate temperatures. Alaska duck hunters should plan on plenty of both and

dress accordingly, with polypropelene underwear and layers of wool topped by high quality rain gear. Neoprene chest waders are comfortable when setting out decoys or waiting in blinds, but since a lot of Alaska duck hunting requires hiking, I usually opt for insulated ankle-fit hip waders instead, even if that means less imaginative decoy spreads.

Then there is the sea—the cold, intimidating North Pacific. While Alaska's interior offers brief periods of superb duck hunting before freeze-up, my most memorable northern duck hunting has taken place on or near saltwater for two reasons: year-round open water means long hunting seasons and the sea sustains an incredible variety of waterfowl. But those waters deserve profound respect. The Coast Guard measures survival time in minutes for victims of boating mishaps in Alaska waters, and even a brief soaking can lead to a critical survival situation if you're not adequately prepared. Two hunting partners and I sank a small boat near Kodiak a few years back and I can assure anyone who cares to hear the story that the swim to shore left a lasting impression.

And don't forget the tides. Cook Inlet has the highest tides in the world outside the Bay of Fundy and rising water can advance faster than a hunter can walk. Hunt in water above the tide line whenever possible, and always know which way the tide is moving and when it's scheduled to turn around and do something else. Be careful where you set your decoys and where you leave your boat. Brief miscalculation can easily lead to a miserable night out in the elements, lost decoys, or worse.

With a little common sense and planning, hunters should be able to keep themselves out of the ocean's clutches, but retrievers are another matter. Bone-chilling water and powerful tidal currents can test any dog to its limits. In fact, Alaska waterfowling reproduces the demanding maritime conditions that led to the

Lab's original development on the Canadian coast centuries ago. But even tough guys can use a little help from their friends. My old friend Bob May handles the hardiest Chesapeake Bay retrievers I know, but on long outings near his Kodiak home, he usually outfits them with neoprene vests. The last time a visiting hunter raised an eyebrow at this practice, Bob politely invited him to jump in and fetch the next duck.

Alaska's wilderness environment creates a unique definition of the ideal retriever in which personality and tractability matter nearly as much as toughness. Doing anything worthwhile out-doors in Alaska usually requires leaving the comfort of home behind, and that means sharing close quarters with companions human and canine, in airplanes, boats and cabins, where unruly dogs wear out their welcome quickly. Tight spaces magnify the effect of bad manners on the part of all company whether it walks on two legs or four. Many Alaskan Lab enthusiasts look for dogs on the small side. Despite my general preference for big, blocky dogs, I have to acknowledge the wisdom of this principle for one simple reason. Every ten pounds of Labrador retriever in the back of a light airplane represents ten pounds of something else you have to leave behind.

Horizontal rain, hypothermia, raging tides… and we haven't even dealt with the bears. At some point, level-headed hunters are bound to ask: why bother? While the pace of the shooting is seldom predictable, it can occasionally be as fast and furious as it gets. Alaska offers a tremendous variety of waterfowl, from regulation issue mallards and Canadas to harlequins, old squaws, eiders and emperor geese. Alaska waterfowling can often be combined with the world-class pursuit of something else, from rainbows and silver salmon early in the season to halibut, caribou and blacktail deer later on.

But in the end, my affection for the Far North always comes back to the love of wild places, one commodity that Alaska alone among the fifty states offers in nearly limitless supply.

A nd finally, a tip of the hat to my favorite dogs' rival breed…

As much as I love my Labs, and as much as I've enjoyed needling my Chessie-owning friends over the years, an admission: no breed of hunting dog seems so perfectly suited to coastal Alaska's unique demands as the Chesapeake Bay retriever. And right along beside me sits my old buddy Yaeger, here tonight to prove it

In a sense, I've misspoken. Chessies never really sit beside you. As far as they're concerned, proximity between man and dog remains a coincidence at best and at worst an inconvenience to be endured until the shooting starts. On temporary assignment from my friend Bob May, Yaeger has followed me down the long winding trail to the cove on the west end of Whale Island not

because he likes me, but because I'm the evening's most likely source of a retrieve. Since I've spent countless hours with Yaeger over the years—in boats, blinds, and even in the kitchen back at Bob's Whale Pass Lodge—I've probably earned the right to take offense at his diffidence. But I still appreciate the uncompromising honesty that has evolved over the course of our relationship. I shoot, he fetches; it's as simple as that. Besides, if Whale Island's resident ten-foot brown bear decides to make an appearance during the long hike home in the dark, I've never met a dog I'd rather have running interference.

Bob breeds his dogs Alaska tough. A few years back, Coco—Yaeger's female kennel-mate—bailed off the back of the boat undetected while Bob was fishing long miles from home. After searching the area unsuccessfully for days, Bob reluctantly gave her up for dead. Two weeks later she showed up at the door, having found her way down countless miles of uninhabited coastline and crossed the channel between Whale Island and the Kodiak mainland, one of the most intimidating reaches of water on earth. A fully equipped team of Navy SEALS would have been hard pressed to duplicate this feat, but Coco hadn't lost a pound. We later hypothesized that she survived by chasing brown bears off deer they'd killed.

The tide is falling tonight. I pitched the decoys out as far as possible from the shoreline, but the water has already started to abandon the spread, and some of the blocks are bouncing against the beach gravel by the time the first set of birds appears around the point. Faintly audible above the breeze, their rhythmic whistling identifies them as goldeneyes even at a distance. The tidally compromised decoy spread might not look like much to a critical eye, but it's enough to earn a fly-by from the birds, whose opinion, after all, is the only one that really counts. At the sound of the shot the lead drake tumbles and I ignore the rest. With the current kicking offshore, one bird is enough even for a dog like Yaeger.

Who, as usual, makes it all look easy. By the time he catches up to the fallen drake, the current has left him a long, hard pull against the tide. But when he finally arrives back at my side, he spits the bird out and retires to his spot in the logs with less fanfare than a backyard dummy would generate from one of my Labs. With daylight draining from the sky I could stand a little canine bonding, but Yaeger apparently has a headache. You want something from me, his yellow eyes seem to say, quit carrying on and shoot another duck.

Not a very Lab-like attitude to be sure, but given our circumstances, just what we need to get us through the afternoon. Alaska is hard country all right, populated by hard dogs and hard people. But it used to be home and it still calls me back as often as I can go. I hope friends like Yaeger will always be there waiting.

The Barley Field

The best laid plans of dogs and men...

My initial encounter with the barley field resulted from serendipitous intelligence. I'd called out to an old friend's place to confirm pheasant hunting permission for my parents' upcoming annual October visit and received the usual clearance. After a pleasant chat with the lady of the ranch about a few minor medical matters, she allowed that she hadn't been getting much sleep lately. Still in clinical mode, I asked if she'd been under any undue stress. "Everything's fine," she assured me with a laugh. "It's just all these damn geese!"

Needless to say, my attitude shifted immediately. In response to further interrogation, she explained that a late summer hail-storm had pounded one of their barley fields and the local waterfowl had discovered the bonanza of fallen grain. And she not only granted permission to set up in the field; she made it clear that as far as she was concerned, we were welcome to kill them all.

That afternoon, Lori and I set out beneath a blustery layer of clouds to scout. Since I wanted to leave the pheasants undis-turbed for my parents, I didn't even take a shotgun. We found no geese in the field, which didn't surprise me given the time of day, but the thin skiff of snow that had fallen that morning bore countless goose tracks. And as we climbed back into the truck to head home, waves of mallards began to appear overhead, spiraling down toward the field like attacking fighter planes. "This," I bravely predicted to Lori, "is going to be a slam dunk." In retrospect, it's easy to say I should have known better.

At quarter-to-dawn the following morning, Lori, Ray Stalmaster and I offloaded a truck-full of decoys and two pop-up blinds and went to work in the dark. One can debate the necessity of dogs when field-shooting geese, but Ray and I each had a youngster in need of work—my Rocky and Alpheus, his Chessie. We'd mutually agreed to put up with the possibility of canine shenanigans in order to advance the dogs' education, and the pair romped happily while we set out the shells and erected the blinds. With our preparations complete and the truck hidden back in the brush at last, we settled in to wait.

The front that had lowered the ceiling and brought the snow the day before had abandoned us, and the sun rose to a clear, still sky better suited to trout fishing than goose hunting. I had to admit that our blinds looked distinctly out of place in the barren field, which my friends had harvested for fodder. But no one had hunted these birds before, and counting on their naivety and numbers, I offered a bold prediction: three easy limits of mallards and a good look at a lot of honkers by mid-morning.

Despite the furious shooting well-chosen grain fields can offer, I've always preferred to set up over water, and after two hours of dead silence overhead I began to remember why. Even in trivial amounts, water concentrates wildlife and encourages biodiversity. Idle time spent beside decoys on creeks or potholes always seems to offer an opportunity to look at something interesting: raptors, muskrats, the inevitable hieroglyphics of sign in the mud underfoot. Stubble fields, on the other hand, remind me of our species' gravest attempts to impose our own idea of order on nature, the very thing that got Ahab into so much trouble aboard the Pequod. As a resident of an area dependent upon an agricultural economy, I appreciate their necessity, and grain fields have certainly served wildlife well enough in their own way. Nonetheless, they don't offer much to arouse one's natural curiosity, a shortcoming most noticeable when the birds you've come for choose to stand you up.

But learning to wait remains an essential part of the waterfowler's character. The still air's splendid acoustics promised plenty of auditory warning from the geese, leaving us free to lounge outside the confinement of the blinds while we caught up on a long September's worth of hunting stories. Alpheus' presence compromised Rocky's ordinarily impeccable blind manners to some degree, but given the comic relief the dogs provided, it was hard to worry too much about lapses in canine discipline. Granted, Ray quizzed me a few more times than necessary about all the ducks overhead and goose sign underfoot we'd seen on our scouting mission the day before, but my assurances seemed to mollify him, especially since Lori—always regarded as less prone to exaggeration than me—confirmed my account. Then suddenly at nine o'clock—just as predicted, I had to point out—we heard the first distant gabble of geese.

Talk about an instant change in ambience… Whistling at the dogs and chambering shells, we scrambled for the security of the blinds. Already experienced enough to know what was up, Rocky began to scan the skies while a chorus of goose talk built to a slow crescendo somewhere to the east. "Birds!" I hissed unnecessarily as the first undulating line of silhouettes appeared against the sun, and for one brief moment I began to feel like a genius.

My triumph proved short lived. Rising from a pond unknown

to any of us despite decades afield in the county, the birds circled noisily and departed to the south as if our decoys and the fallen barley beneath them didn't exist. In the silence that followed, even Rocky looked as if he'd been cheated. "We're screwed," Ray observed simply, and absent any attempt at argument we emerged from the blinds to begin the laborious process of undoing all we had done a few hours before. "I saw some geese on a pond north of town the other day," Ray said as he heaved the last decoy bag into the truck. "Give me a call tonight and we'll make a plan. I'm dying to get you back for this one."

I didn't doubt him for a second.

W riters, alas, must bear their share of blame for waterfowling's Grand Illusion: that effort will always lead to just reward. Disputing this principle seems downright un-American, but we all know better, no one more than me. For every morning I've spent reloading furiously, I've spent many more shivering in silence. And my most frustrating whiffs often follow the greatest investments of time and energy, especially in the pursuit of geese, whose very nature invites this kind of comeuppance.

Lack of shooting while hunting ducks and geese differs fundamentally from slow upland gunning. After hiking an hour or two without flushing a pheasant, the dogs and I still know just what to do: gird up our loins and hit the cover a little harder. Waterfowling, on the other hand—at least over decoys, as I prefer it—leaves little choice in the face of miscalculation other than to sit and take the consequences. In this respect, the pursuit of waterfowl resembles bowhunting, another mentally demanding discipline that has taught me plenty about getting through days that don't turn out as planned.

The trick is to regard the process as more important than the result. Granted, it helps to have the process include some snappy doubles and soul-stirring dog work eventually, but that isn't always going to be the case. Rather than fidgeting impatiently in duck blinds on slow mornings, I prefer to concentrate on what's still there: sunrises, the absence of telephones, the eager look in the dogs' eyes as they study the sky overhead. Training yourself to believe there's no such thing as a bad day of hunting creates a self-fulfilling prophecy.

And when all else fails, it helps to remember that Samuel Beckett's most enduring play concerns a long wait for nothing, and they gave him the Nobel Prize for Literature. Sometimes I have to wonder if Beckett wrote *Waiting for Godot* in a duck blind.

Just as patience and optimism are essential to the waterfowler, so is persistence. Three days after our Great Bloodless Goose Shoot, I left work early thinking about the waves of mallards Lori and I had seen barreling into the barley field the afternoon we'd scouted the place. Oddly enough, I couldn't talk either Ray or Lori into a return trip, so I loaded Rocky into the rig and set off with no company other than the dog. I never really felt confidence in our blinds that first morning, but I'd noticed a pair of wheels on an irrigation rig alongside the field that looked like a natural framework for a blind. After scattering some duck

decoys around the stubble, I stretched a piece of netting across the wheels and Rocky and I settled in to become part of the landscape.

Nothing establishes the value of a pleasant canine personality like confinement in a blind on a slow day. Demonstrating boundless enthusiasm without becoming a pain in the ass can be a tough trick, but with no other dogs around to distract him, Rocky showed that he'd mastered the art like a natural. My single raised forefinger anchored him to the ground beneath the netting. From there, his eyes swept the sky like radar, and I had to admit that his confidence in my judgment appeared to exceed my own. No fidgeting, no questions, no second thoughts… all the social graces one could ask for in a hunting companion.

The landowner had moved cattle that day, leaving calves on the opposite side of a fence from their mothers for the first time in their lives. None of the parties seemed happy about the situation, and for two hours mournful bovine lowing filled the air.

Determined to leave the pheasant cover untouched for my folks, I resisted the urge to dispel the tedium by running the dog through the cattails along the nearby creek. If Rocky resented this decision, he remained too polite to comment.

Finally, the rich, rolling chuckle of inbound mallards rose above the sound of the cattle. Rocky already had the birds in sight. Following his gaze to the north, I saw waves of ducks above the cottonwoods along the creek and squirmed into ready position. Moments later, the sound of air tearing through extended primaries filled the air. The first flock made a low pass just out of range, climbed, and circled to join the next arrivals in a gathering vortex that eventually swelled to hundreds. Face turned upward, Rocky remained transfixed, moving nothing but his eyes while I waited for part of the milling mass to pass within range.

But that didn't happen. I've never understood how decisions are made within large flocks of ducks, especially under such chaotic circumstances. Acting according to some communal will, the mob ignored the decoys and drifted off slowly to the south, feinting repeatedly at the field without ever committing to land. When the flock finally disappeared from sight, I rose and stretched my cramped leg muscles and invited Rocky to do the same. For the second time in a row, the barley field remained a promise unfulfilled.

We finally enjoyed our redemption. I'd noted that many of the ducks working the field had circled a small, spring-fed pond along its southern edge. I set a dozen decoys on its surface the next afternoon, blocks that looked like ducks instead of something the cows had left behind in the stubble. When the

waves of mallards arrived once more, enough circled overhead
with wings set to provide me an easy limit me and Rocky five
welcome retrieves.

But contrary to convention, I'm not going to dwell on the
excitement of the birds overhead, the shooting, or the geyser of
spray Rocky generated with each water entry. There will always
be time for such discussions. What intrigued me about the barley
field was the extent of the challenge it provided. Aldo Leopold
once noted that the value of a trophy depends directly upon the
amount of effort invested in obtaining it. By this sensible standard, the mallards I carried home that day felt as satisfying as a
bull elk.

As I crossed a corner of the field on my way back to the
truck, a flicker of reflected sunlight caught my eye in the dirt
underfoot. Moments later, I stood admiring the partly fractured
remains of an exquisite flint arrowhead. Leave it to history to
put contemporary issues into perspective. When the game out-
witted me, I went home and took something out of the freezer,
an option unavailable to my anonymous Paleolithic predecessor
when he stalked the valley countless years before. If nothing else,
the stone point reminded me that, win or lose, we've all been at
this for a hell of a long time.

With that, I whistled to the dog and left the barley field
behind.

Field and Stream

Two ways to shoot geese, with dogs essential to both

Although it was still early October, ice tinkled beneath our waders as Ray Stalmaster and I slogged across the edge of the marsh to place the decoys while Sky and Lester, Ray's Chessie, splashed along the shoreline with unfocused enthusiasm. All this seemed like a lot of industry to bring to bear upon a two acre wet spot in the absolute middle of nowhere, but no facet of outdoor sport breeds optimism quite like goose hunting.

Once we had the blocks distributed to our liking, we retired to the cattails to sit and shiver as dawn broke slowly in the eastern sky. By the time the light introduced the first blush of color to the landscape, the air felt warm enough to let us enjoy the spectacle of a brilliant prairie sunrise. Marsh birds began to stir in the reeds. A pair of coots materialized on the water and worked their way around the edge of our spread in their own ungainly fashion. Finally a flock of teal appeared over the end of the pond, heading erratically toward the decoys.

"What do you think?" Ray whispered eagerly.

"We might spook the geese," I pointed out.

"Aw, hell," Ray replied. "Let's take 'em." And we did, rising over the top of the reeds and picking out birds as they flared on either side of us. Moments later, three blue-wings lay kicking their last on the surface of the pond as the dogs sent geysers of swamp water flying in all directions. That's one of the reasons I love hunting with Ray. If it's legal and looks like fun, he's never one to stand on ceremony.

"We had to do it for the dogs," Ray explained as he ejected his empties. "Look how happy they are out there!" As excuses for discipline breakdowns go, I'm not sure I've ever heard a better one.

As it turned out, our intemperance with the teal cost us nothing. Nearly two hours passed before the first sound of geese rose above the breeze. While Ray urged the dogs to the blind's muddy floor, I began to call, and moments later the geese were losing altitude and descending in our direction. Although they were still a half-mile away, I knew in my heart that we had them.

The sense of anticipation produced by an inbound flock of geese reminds me of hunting big game. After a minute or two watching honkers approach a decoy spread, my hands start to shake as they do when I'm watching a big whitetail ooze into bow range or bugling in a bull elk. That is what you come for, the moment when you realize that your strategies have worked and nature is about to serve you up an opportunity to make or squander. All of us could feel it, even the dogs. And then the leading edge of the flight was hanging above the decoys and Ray and I were on our feet picking out birds and swinging our guns all over again.

But these birds weren't teal. When I rise to address a flock of geese, I'm always amazed to discover how far away they really are, and how fast they're flying. It took me a moment to get the gun out in front of the first bird and when I slapped the trigger, the goose tumbled with a broken wing and little else. By that time, more birds were flaring right overhead and my second barrel dropped one with a splat that sounded as if a meteor had hit the mud behind the blind.

Lester scooped Ray's first bird from the decoy spread while I gave Sky a line on my cripple. No more impressed by protocol than his handler, Lester broke and set out behind him, but I didn't mind. Sky was a highly experienced retriever, but a crippled goose sometimes calls for all the help a dog can get.

We marked their progress by the motion of the reeds. Finally, Sky emerged from the cover at the edge of the pond and disappeared into a brushy draw with Lester right behind him. Moments later, a chorus of howls rose from the bushes and I wondered if one of the dogs had stepped in a leg hold trap. In fact, they had run right into a belligerent boar raccoon, which, as houndsmen know, can cause a dog more grief than a mountain lion. When they finally emerged from the brush, Sky was carrying the goose and Lester was carrying the dead raccoon. Oh well; Chessies will always be Chessies.

Half an hour later, we called in another flight of honkers and by the time we finished shooting we had all the geese I wanted to pick even though the dogs looked ready to stay all morning. I usually feel a wistful sense of denouement as I pick up my decoys and stow them away after a hunt, but not this time. The prairie looked too beautiful; the day felt as complete as the company. As much as I enjoy my solitude, friends always lend a special measure of satisfaction to the hunting experience.

Friends, human and otherwise…

In my own simplistic view, there are basically two places to shoot geese: where they eat and where they live. Those hunting geese near wintering grounds generally prefer the former for practical reasons. Shooting geese over their home water tends to unsettle the birds and disrupt their daily movement patterns, while honkers that have faced fire over fields just move to another square on the chessboard the following day. In my country such concerns aren't a big issue, because our geese are usually in transit and the most practical place to set up a goose shoot lies wherever you happen to find the birds.

In fact, I prefer shooting geese over water for a variety of reasons. Ponds and marshes provide a convenient array of blind options, while digging pits in frozen fields challenges the distinction between sport and work. Retrievers always look happiest when they're dripping wet. Finally, prairie marshes are interesting places, full of the kind of wildlife that makes time pass easily whether you're listening to blackbirds, watching raptors overhead, or shooting wayward teal. All that matters to me, even though I know I'd shoot more geese if it didn't.

No matter what the setting, I've always enjoyed goose hunting and wish I had an opportunity to do more of it. I appreciate the challenge of the birds' wariness and the anticipation of their long approach to the decoys. I love the way they crash when they hit the ground and the Look at this! expression on the dog's face at the end of each retrieve. And if experiencing all these rewards requires abandoning water for the relative sterility of a frozen field, so be it.

The prairie can become downright cruel by the end of the calendar year, when the landscape looks like a washed out photograph of a place you wouldn't want to visit and the wind cuts to the bone. As we bounce along in the darkness, I can imagine a long list of pleasures I will not be enjoying over the course of the next few hours. My only hope is that by the time we're done, this list will not include shooting geese.

Our friend Tom Budde has them located, or so he says. The problem is that Tom can get lost on a road that runs in only two directions and we've been rattling across trackless stubble fields for nearly an hour. When we pull to a stop, Lori and I exchange worried looks as Tom roots around in the dirt outside the truck. Finally he rises with a smile of triumph plastered across his face and a frozen goose turd between his fingers. We have arrived.

I'll give Tom credit for the blinds, elaborately woven rolls of wire mesh and grass that look enough like shocks of wheat straw to stand a chance of letting us get away with what we are about to try. But I also know we're hunting educated late season geese and that there aren't going to be a lot of legs dangling in the decoys. The best we can hope for is a low level fly-by, but at least we didn't have to dig any pits.

With the blinds set up and the decoys distributed, I volunteer to move the truck back to the shelter of the nearest coulee. This precipitates the recurring argument that always takes place when

we shoot geese in fields. Ray wants to keep Lester in the blind.
Tom insists that a dog will prove nothing but a useless in such
open terrain. Lori makes it plain that she wants no part of this
dispute. Faced with the responsibility of the tie-breaking vote, I
compromise my principles in deference to the fact that it's Tom's
hunt, and if one of the dogs screws up, I won't want to hear
about it. One of these days, I'm going to learn.

I'm right about one thing: there isn't much to look at when
the sun rises today. When you say the word *nothing* in this country at this time of year, you really should spell it with a capital N.
No birds, no animals, no insects; just cold sky, an endless sea of
wheat stubble, and a few scattered patches of snow. We might as
well be looking out the window of a lunar landing craft.

After two cold, lonely hours, we're ready to pack up and leave
when we hear geese off to the south. Goose talk always sounds
deceptive, since a few vocal honkers can make a tremendous
racket. But this morning's rich chorus of voices makes it obvious

that we're listening to birds numbering in the hundreds if not the thousands, an impression soon confirmed by lines of geese rising above the distant Missouri. Harassed all morning, Tom turns and smiles in vindication. Nothing doesn't look quite so empty anymore.

As the birds gain altitude and disperse toward the fields, we all call furiously. One flight turns in our direction, but it's hard to feel the kind of conviction I feel when I'm set up over water. Countless stubble fields lie scattered about the area, none of which sport bogus eight-foot piles of straw. All we have to sustain our hope is Tom's scouting and a few goose droppings underfoot. At this point, that will just have to do.

Our spread earns us one good look, but that is enough. After the inevitable confusion over when to stand and shoot, we all somehow get to our feet at the same time and the sky begins to rain geese. Several guns working translates into a lot of shooting over a short period of time, during which I spot at least one cripple waddling off across the field to the west.

Ignoring the racket, a small flock follows immediately after the first, and by the time we're done with them it's impossible to keep track of who has shot what, except that none of us has fired enough shells to exceed a limit. With waves of birds still in the air, I call time out to collect what's on the ground. While Lori, Ray and I pick up dead birds from the decoys, Tom runs down one long cripple and dispatches it on the ground. But when we regroup at the blind, our math doesn't hold up. There are three possible explanations. Someone may have failed to admit a miss. We could have double-shot more birds than we realized. Or we may have lost a bird out there somewhere.

"Let's go back and get the dogs," Ray suggests. Lines of

geese still undulate through the air over the river. We're a long way from filling our generous modern limits. But we all know what honor requires.

Twenty minutes later, Ray and I are following Sonny and Lester down the grassy swale on the far side of the stubble field when both dogs begin to make game. Then Lester pounces into the dry grass and it's over. The geese in the air to the south no longer matter. We have what counts—the honor of completing the hunt with no lost birds—and with the last of the morning flights disappearing into the cold winter sky, we head back to begin the process of breaking down the blinds.

B y virtue of both cunning and size, Canada geese really are the wingshooter's answer to big game. You can measure this conviction by the impression the birds leave after the shooting is done. Ducks tend to blend together in the memory once you've plucked and devoured them, but geese, like antelope and elk, live on. And at the risk of sounding hopelessly sentimental, I'll go on record as believing my Labs think so too. You can sense it in the way they struggle to control their excitement when geese are in the air and the way they act as if they've done something special when they deliver a fallen bird to your hand.

No matter where you shoot your geese, good dogs belong at your side. Make them part of the team and they'll never let you forget why.

Snow Falling on Mallards

And, we hope, mallards falling on snow

You just can't do late season greenheads right without a Labrador retriever. When (and if) the shooting starts, the obvious reason will become just that, but Sonny's importance here this morning extends beyond practicalities. No element of the outdoor experience enforces the value of companionship like cold weather, and I don't need a thermometer to confirm that the arctic high parked over the valley all week means business. Snow crunches underfoot and branches crack in the cottonwoods overhead. The brush along the creek stands gilded by complex layers of ice crystals. This morning's cold isn't one of those inflated chill-factor propositions. The wind velocity stands at zero. If only the temperature would rise to the same.

But for some reason, duck blinds always seem warmer with a dog inside them, even when the dog is fresh from the creek. You'd think that after all these seasons Sonny would know enough to stay ashore until ducks start dropping, but that kind of common sense would represent a betrayal of the Labrador retriever's view of life, according to which God made water for Labs to swim in. This perverse canine instinct already translated into plenty of less than welcome assistance as I set the decoys out. But I knew enough to dodge that first frantic shake back on the bank, and the weather took care of the rest. As we settle into our little blind at the edge of the willows, the water on his coat has already turned to ice, rendering the moisture from the creek harmless to bystanders.

All serious waterfowlers eventually master the art of waiting, at least if they appreciate the spectacle of ducks settling into decoys. But sub-zero weather raises the discipline required to unprecedented levels. There's enough raw beauty in the winter landscape surrounding us to make the first half hour pass easily enough, but then the relentless progression of discomfort begins. As always, the feet protest first, for insulated waders and multiple layers of socks can only delay the inevitable. Foot stomping and toe wiggling help, but not nearly enough. The face goes next. My ski mask keeps the chill at bay for a while, but eventually the condensation from my breath turns mask and beard into a miserable, cohesive chunk of ice. Finally, a self-imposed ultimatum: if the birds don't show up within the next twenty minutes, they can have the creek to themselves for the rest of the day.

The physics are simple: cold air carries sound louder and more clearly than warm air because its molecules lie crowded closer together. Sometimes the acoustics of late season duck hunting can be even more dramatic than the sights, as is the case this morning. Five minutes before the deadline for withdrawal, a rich wave of mallard chuckles breaks over the hills to the south and when I finally spot the birds, it's shocking to realize how far away they actually are. But there's only one place left in the frozen valley to accommodate them, and we are sitting right beside it.

Of course there's miles of creek for them to choose from, but I've done my scouting and the decoys bobbing in the current should take care of any last minute indecision on the part of the birds. Cold feet forgotten, I'm concentrating on a small flock circling upstream when a vast wave of wings breaks over the trees from the opposite direction. Despite the crush of mallards overhead, my shotgun only holds two shells, and the objective is to convert each of them into a cleanly killed drake. The rest of the ducks are nothing more than part of the show, an important point to keep in mind when it comes time to rise, isolate two targets, and fire.

It's hard to explain the self-imposed importance I feel about selectively shooting mallard drakes. There are legal considerations, of course: Central Flyway limits allow five mallards only two of which can be hens. But I'd certainly prefer that all five of my birds—should it come to that—have green heads. I don't think it matters much biologically and hens taste just as good as drakes, but there's something visually compelling about five plump greenheads lying together in the snow at the end of a long, cold morning, and when you're surrounded by birds, you ought to be able to pick the ones you really want to kill.

An admission: shooting ducks hanging over a spread of decoys twenty yards away should be a wingshooter's mulligan, but I've always found those shots surprisingly difficult. Correct technique, of course, is simply to mount the gun, point it and fire, as if you were exterminating gophers in the back yard. But I find it practically impossible to shoot a shotgun without swinging, a deeply ingrained habit that serves well on all targets other than hovering ducks. I've learned to solve the problem by taking incoming ducks a lot farther out than necessary, when they still have some airspeed beneath their wings. While this approach requires some coordination when I'm sharing a blind with another hunter, it has served me well over many seasons. Besides, there's no one around this morning to offend by rising early other than the dog.

As a dozen birds peel out of the milling flock and begin their descent toward the water, I'm busy isolating the two I plan to take. At close range in good light, a drake mallard's signature green head appears obvious. But when the birds are well overhead where I prefer to shoot them, I find it easier to look for the sharp demarcation between the drakes' dark thorax and light abdomen, an easily recognized field mark absent in hens. That much settled, the shooting itself is over in seconds, illustrating once again how little of the hunting process actually involves killing game. And finally—according to Sonny—it's time for the dog.

Drake number one lies stone dead across the creek, its resting place marked distinctly by an entrance wound in a freshly windblown bank of snow. But the second bird is bobbing away downstream like a discarded beer can, and that's the one that demands the dog's attention first. After giving Sonny the line, I settle back and watch him run the bank downstream, a lapse of protocol I freely encourage when hunting moving water, where one must learn to bend some rules. His eventual entry—a full speed, extended swan dive off a six-foot bank—looks like a performance in some canine Olympic event. Five minutes later we're back in the willows where we started, watching the two dead drakes turn into feathered ice cubes and waiting for the next set to arrive.

Oddly enough, I've forgotten all about my cold feet, even though the thermometer hasn't budged at all.

Hunting late-season mallards provides a quirky epilogue to our duck season here on the high plains. Trout streams at heart, our local creeks lack the panoramic big-water feel of traditional duck marshes. The early season's great mixed flights are long gone, leaving nothing but mallards behind. Rich autumn foliage has yielded to the black-and-white world of winter. Sometimes the cold proves unbearable. But I can't imagine the week between Christmas and New Year without dog and shotgun.

Part of the late season's appeal derives from the calendar. With big game and upland bird seasons recently completed, the urge to be afield persists—at least for me—even as the options there diminish. There's a delicious loneliness to most of the hunting, since setting out decoys in sub-zero weather isn't an activity that draws a lot of crowds. And winter landscapes can certainly be beautiful in their own right, even if that beauty can be difficult to appreciate once you lose all feeling in your toes.

But winter mallard hunting finally boils down to an intimate dialog between hunter and quarry. Few settings offer the opportunity to be so close, so suddenly, to so many ducks. Despite the discomfort it can cause, cold drives the whole show as it concentrates the birds on spring-fed creeks and ponds capable of resisting winter's icy grip. Hence an essential paradox: the nicer the weather, the slower the shooting. And vice versa, which explains my enthusiasm for setting up on bitter mornings.

While shooting over decoys represents the best way to appreciate late season mallards, I'm hardly above an occasional jump-shooting expedition, as a favor to the dog, when we need a few birds for an unplanned dinner, or on warmer days when the ducks just aren't moving. I know several small springs with good approaches that would allow me to reach slam-dunk range of dozens of birds with minimal effort, but that kind of shooting doesn't appeal to me much anymore, and when I visit those secret places I'm usually carrying a camera rather than a shotgun. The local creeks and rivers are another matter. The birds soon learn to avoid high banks that eclipse their vision, making long belly-crawls through the snow toward wary flocks of mallards as challenging as stalking antelope.

Whatever the method, the rewards of being in the right place

at the right time extend beyond the shooting. Early season mallard hunting can be all kinds of fun, but the birds themselves often disappoint, providing fluff rather than heft in the hand and an inevitable sub-carpet of pin feathers when plucked. But by December, the birds have outgrown those shortcomings. They feel like prizes when the dog delivers them and wild duck rarely gets better on the table.

Those who know enough to appreciate any species at its finest, rest assured. These are mallards at their best.

And finally, a tip of the hat to the dogs. Much as I love eating mallards, I doubt I'd walk across the yard to shoot one if I couldn't bring a Lab along. Shooting birds at close range over decoys isn't particularly difficult, but the dog work that follows often proves spectacular. Eager retrievers plunging into icy water appeal straight to the heart. On cold December mornings I can't imagine leaving home without one.

Despite an hour's worth of empty skies, I know the mallards will come eventually. The only question is whether they will arrive before or after the end of legal shooting light. The previous afternoon, after a long cougar chase that came to nothing in the mountains to the south, I parked the truck on the way home and glassed the valley at last light until I saw the birds returning to the river from the fields in waves, and this is the pool they wanted. Dependent upon my second-hand intelligence, Lori lacks my conviction, but it's a balmy afternoon by local standards and the waiting feels almost as relaxed as the company: just the two of us and Rocky. Intent beyond his years, he's still studying the sky long after his alleged overseers have lapsed into idle conversation.

Finally, I notice the dog's attention fixed high downriver and track his gaze with my own eyes. At first, the birds look like a pall of smoke rising from the stubble fields, but before we've finished scrambling through our last minute preparations for their arrival, we can appreciate the warm afternoon sunlight flashing off their primaries, and then the sound of setting wings splitting the air.

"Told you so," I whisper to Lori as we brace to rise.

"I'm so lucky I'm married to you," she responds with what sounds suspiciously like sarcasm. But then the ducks start barreling in through the tops of the cottonwoods, eliminating any possibility of marital discord.

Another promise fulfilled, another reason to appreciate the best company imaginable: my wife and my dog.

ROCKY

New Lab puppies arrive in the household by one of several means. Sometimes they're the product of an in-house breeding to a dam you own, in which case you had best be mentally prepared for weeks' worth of very busy company. Even if you don't own Mom, other pups arrive with a certain sense of familiarity, as the product of breedings you have helped arrange, with one or both parents well known to you. If a dog of your own has sired the litter, the pup will carry the burden of fairly precise expectations, standards to which the youngster may or may not eventually rise. Then there's the pig-in-a-poke approach, with pups chosen solely on the basis of advice, recommendation, and the scrutiny of bloodlines. It's important to jump off this cliff from time to time in order to keep the kennel fresh and vibrant, but there's always a certain amount of trepidation involved, like opening the door at the beginning of a blind date.

Whatever the mechanism, taking on the responsibility of a new pup always represents a major commitment. No matter how many times I've been through the process, I'm always amazed by the genuine emotional excitement I still feel every time we welcome a new puppy into the home. Comparisons to the birth of a child may seem hyperbolic, but only to those who don't appreciate the enduring value of a good Labrador retriever.

Rocky arrived by the third route, an import from the Midwest. My decision to reach out for some new blood involved complex factors beyond the scope of this discussion, but I knew it was time for a change. When you already enjoy the company of an excellent canine hunting companion, it's easy to succumb to the fiction that the relationship will last forever, unfortunately a biologic impossibility. I learned that lesson years ago when Sky hit the wall of advancing age and I had no suitable replacement. Ever since, I've made a point to maintain a regular succession of hunting dogs spaced at intervals of approximately three years. It pays to err on the safe side, since some dogs don't work out, accidents happen, and the thought of an autumn without a working Lab at my side would be unbearable.

I don't offer my experiences with Rocky during the first two years of his life as any sort of ideal standard, either in my approach to his training or its result. But we've had some great times together already, and the experiences we've shared illustrate the unique bonds that develop between Labs and hunting families.

So come on along and meet the new kid on the block.

The Age of Innocence

Enter Rocky

Always an important event when a new puppy arrives in the household, the selection of a name marks the dog's transition from the anonymous product of a pedigree to part of the family. There's little reason involved in the choice and the dog's eventual performance in the field can't possibly depend on what you decide to call it. But naming a dog remains an intensely personal process, and I'm sure I've put as much effort into naming puppies as I have into naming my own kids, for more or less the same reasons.

This time around, my absence from town at the time of the new puppy's arrival complicated matters considerably. Few wait to see a child born before deciding on a name or at least a roster of possibilities, but dogs are different. Notions may occur in advance, but I'm never sure of my choice until I've rolled around on the floor with the new addition to the kennel and smelled that great new puppy smell. Imagine giving a name like Corky, Buck, or Mike to an obvious Ranger. That kind of error could create a lifetime of dissonance.

This time around, I was off on an assignment in the wilds of Labrador (appropriately enough) by the time breeders Jim and Victoria Keldsen finally worked the pup through the increasingly convoluted workings of the airline system, all the way from Indiana to Montana. Lori was certainly capable of receiving the

dog in my absence, but I fretted almost unreasonably about our lack of a name. A young pup recently separated from mother and littermates and shipped halfway across the continent shouldn't have to spend much time in a new home without an identity of its own.

In fact, we had discussed some ideas prior to my departure. I'd suggested Gao in honor of a Bushman tracker we'd befriended during a month in the Kalahari, but as Lori correctly pointed out, that sounded prohibitively like No and might create an unnecessary source of confusion. Teenaged daughter Nicole offered several suggestions derived from the names of bands that produce wretched music, but I invoked executive privilege to veto them all.

"Take a look at the pup, get to know him, and pick something," I finally said as I set off for my faraway appointment with brook trout and caribou.

When I finally found my way back to a telephone a week later, my first call home naturally began with an inquiry about the puppy. (By this time, I'd decided the kids could take care of themselves). He had indeed arrived safe and sound, and the background noise over the telephone made it clear that the kids were already spoiling him rotten. "Have you picked a name?" I finally asked.

"Right now, it seems to be No No Bad Dog," Lori explained.

"Don't tell me he chewed up one of the bear rugs," I replied apprehensively.

"He tried, but I caught him in time. Of course, he's not really bad. He's just… busy."

"Sounds like a normal Lab puppy," I sighed with relief. "But he's eight weeks old and he needs a name."

"Unless you want to authorize Nicole…"

"I don't," I interrupted quickly.

"Then you'll have to name him when you get back." And that was the end of the discussion.

As soon as I walked through the doorway two days later, a miniature yellow missile hurtled past old Sonny (no difficult accomplishment by then) and collided with my shins. First things first: I could kiss Lori and talk to the kids when time allowed. Dropping my duffel, I lay prone and let the dog lick my face and plant his cold nose against my neck. Rolling onto my back, I closed my eyes and let him sniff me as I sniffed in return and forgave the insistent tug of teeth against my beard. Finally I rose to my knees to enjoy my first good look at my next life project. "Rocky!" I suddenly blurted as if in response to divine inspiration.

"Rocky?" Nicole repeated aghast, as only teenage girls can

respond to parental suggestion. But no other opinion mattered anymore… the name had declared itself. For a moment I tried to pretend the hard part was over, even though I knew better.

J ake treated Rocky the way he treats everything else he can't retrieve: like a soccer ball. Although strikingly good looking and pleasant enough in his own enthusiastic way, Jake has never been a particularly affectionate dog and he remains one of the few Labs I've owned who has never enjoyed full run of the house. Difficulty sharing feelings with others, a therapist's notes might read. While I'll admit a bit of disappointment over Jake's emotional detachment, his enthusiasm for cold water retrieves earns him plenty of redemption between October and January. At any rate, his response to the new pup afforded few surprises. Jake ran over Rocky the same way he runs over everything standing between him and where he wants to be, and that was pretty much the end of it.

Sonny's response proved more complex from the start, and little wonder. For over a decade, Sonny had reigned supreme over

the house, quietly (and sometimes not so quietly) lording it over an assortment of lesser retrievers, bird dogs, hounds and other canines who never quite made it to the Inner Circle, at least not the same way Sonny did. A certain amount of jealousy seemed inevitable. To complicate matters further, Rocky seemed to adopt Sonny immediately as a surrogate parent. In contrast to

Jake, Sonny never enjoyed the option of ignoring the puppy, since Rocky focused his attention upon him constantly and Sonny lacked the physical capacity to outrun it.

In light of past events, it was hard not to view Sonny's skepticism with apprehension. When Jake first arrived in the household, Sonny, young and in his physical prime, could scarcely contain his jealousy. One winter day when Jake was still small enough to fit inside a shoebox, Sonny evaded our security measures, led little Jake down into the coulee behind the house, and abandoned him. None of us ever doubted the deliberate nature of this act. After days of dragnet searching, we had all but abandoned the pup for dead when a friend on horseback heard him whining beneath a snow-covered log and rescued him. Needless to say, we weren't about to go through that again.

Fortunately, age had caught up with the perpetrator. I honestly think Sonny tried to lose Rocky a time or two (under my surreptitious observation), but he lacked the stamina to get much past the yard. Within a week, the old guy appeared resigned to his fate, which consisted of enduring hours of harmless mauling courtesy of the puppy while rolling his eyes toward the sky like a martyr. *Can this really be my fate?* he seemed to ask as the puppy chewed his ears and harassed him throughout his daily routine, which by then consisted mostly of long, dedicated naps. *Count on it,* I assured him in return.

But even a patient old-timer like Sonny has his limits, and in any carnivorous species nothing defines those limits as predictably as the defense of a food source. Located on the front porch right outside the kitchen door where it serves as a ready repository for table scraps, Sonny's food dish seemed to hold an endless fascination for the pup even when it contained nothing more interesting than regulation issue dog food. Rocky found the contents of the

dish irresistible no matter what they were, much to Sonny's distress. Anticipating conflict, I watched over these encounters carefully in case resentment escalated to the point of violence.

But Sonny's days of serious belligerence were long past, courtesy of a hound named Drive. In his youth, Sonny was a scrapper
and wouldn't hesitate to pick a fight with any male dog invading
his turf. A rangy blue tick, Drive had the sweetest personality of
any hound I've ever known, a trait Sonny exploited by endless
bullying whenever the two dogs met. Note to Labrador retrievers: pick on cougar hounds at your own risk. One day Drive evidently decided he'd had enough. When Sonny muscled up to
him with a series of menacing growls, Drive knocked him on his
back and seized him by the throat. As I ran over to prevent serious injury, Sonny whined for mercy and assumed the fetal position while Drive looked up apologetically and released him
unharmed. In a matter of seconds, the hound had taught Sonny a
lesson I'd tried to teach him for years, and I never saw him raise
his hackles at another dog again.

Of course he had never had to endure such serious or pro-
longed incitement. But after refereeing a number of these
encounters over the once sacred food dish, it became apparent
that Sonny had reformed for good, either as a function of
advancing age or, as I secretly suspected, reluctant affection for
the puppy. Whatever the case, he tolerated these infringements
upon his personal domain with no real hostility. For a while, he
tried to shield his bowl against the puppy's advances like a line-
man protecting a quarterback, but Rocky was too quick and
determined, leaving Sonny no option other than to stand aside
and howl mournfully until his pint-sized tormentor moved along
to another source of mischief.

In contrast to Jake—a dog people seem to admire more than

like—Rocky demonstrated real charm from the very start. I've always maintained that Labs have a natural affinity for children and Rocky proved no exception. Since I view socialization as the first order of business in a young dog's life, I didn't fret too much over the attention the kids paid him. I did lay down a few ground rules: no physical punishment, contradictory commands, or scolding for anything he did with his mouth. Other than that, they were all free to romp as they saw fit, and did they ever.

Lori's relationship with the pup proved a bit more complicated. Since she serves as the guardian of neatness and order around the house (no surprise to anyone who knows me), the sudden arrival of this energized bundle of chaos challenged her patience from the start. On the other hand, she and Rocky had already formed a special bond by the time I returned from Canada and she forgave his sins with surprising ease. As soon as the nights started to turn crisp, she was always the one who lobbied to let the pup stay inside overnight no matter what the consequences. Of course, the following morning she would point these consequences out to me as well as the pup as if I were the one who was not quite through with my house training. Overall, however, these lectures seemed a small price to pay for the affection that had obviously developed between the two of them and the value of friendly relationships between spouses and hunting dogs should never be underestimated.

Marked by innocence rather than the need to accomplish anything in particular, there's nothing quite like the first few weeks spent adjusting to life with a new puppy. While the satisfaction of sophisticated training will have to wait its turn, the sheer exuberance of a puppy's early integration into the family can challenge and reward all concerned, human and canine alike. And as with raising one's own kids, time seems to pass with disorienting speed. Before we knew it, Rocky had graduated from a squiggling fur ball to Sit, Come, and Heel, at least in elemental form. This meant being called upon to assume some responsibility for his actions, a transition that spells an end to the age of innocence.

Uncharacteristically, I began this essay in its original form after returning from a long September day in the field. After all that sun and dust, the urge to retire at once to the bathtub with a cold beer felt compelling, but I'd been doing a lot of thinking about the dogs as I kicked the cover and I wanted to shape my thoughts before they abandoned me. I took time to let the pup inside though, and for the first thousand words Rocky made polite company beneath my feet as I wrote.

Suddenly I recognized an ominous silence. Distracted by the demands of composition, I'd let the pup weasel out of my den and enter the rest of the house unsupervised. The lack of the usual puppy noises suggested a disaster in progress, and I bolted upstairs to confirm my worst suspicions.

A life-size mount of a bobcat guarding a dead sharptail rests at floor level in our living room, a favorite bit of taxidermy mounted by a close friend and regular hunting partner. The good news was that the pup had ignored the bobcat. The bad news was that he'd found the grouse and dragged it about the house leaving a trail of slobbery feathers in his wake. And there he sat, posed as for a calendar photo with the remains of the bird resting in his eager mouth and a look on his face that practically defied me to feel anger much less express it. And after all, he had a point. He had found the closest thing to a game bird in the house.

Enjoy the Age of Innocence while it lasts.

New Kid on the Block

How much hunt can you ask from a pup?
As much as he wants to give

I n the wake of the season's first real cold snap, I called my old friend Ray Stalmaster and invited him to accompany me to a favorite little spring-fed slough that often fills up with mallards after a hard freeze. Ray had spent the fall aggressively working a new young Chessie on upland game, and I knew how anxious he was to introduce the dog to ducks over decoys. Almost as an afterthought, I asked if he'd mind if I brought Rocky along. Of course, Ray assented even though Rocky was still very much a puppy. We've spent years helping introduce one another's young dogs to the field and each of us owes the other an incalculable debt of patience and understanding in these matters.

I certainly didn't expect anything from the Rocky, who was not quite five months old at the time. But I've always felt it important to introduce dogs to the experience if not the demands of hunting at an early age. I want my pups to know from the start that when the lights go on in the dark and the shotgun comes out of the cabinet, serious fun lies ahead. And so we set off through the snow that morning with a pleasantly diverse mix of job descriptions: I would shoot, Ray would handle his Chessie who would fetch a limit of mallards, and Rocky would enjoy his first introduction to the Big Show.

Of course, seasoned trainers will recognize the presence of two

inexperienced dogs in the same duck blind as a recipe for chaos if
not actual disaster. The first hurdle is psychological: the dogs,
rather than the shooting, have to be the order of the day, and
Ray and I had that much worked out well in advance. And it
helps to have comfortable quarters with plenty of room to spread
out and keep the dogs separated. The little slough fit the bill perfectly, because we could sit in the brush along the bank without
having to worry about crowding into a wet blind. So while I set
out a dozen decoys with the first sound of wings whistling overhead in the darkness, Ray stomped out a nest in the willows and
then we settled in to wait for shooting light.

The morning passed pleasantly if not spectacularly. The big
waves of northern mallards I had anticipated never materialized,
but enough singles and pairs drifted in to provide some shooting
and an opportunity for Ray's dog to work. The young Chessie
performed creditably and Rocky seemed to enjoy the sound of
the shotgun and the smell of the birds as they accumulated in a

pile beneath our feet. The occasionally rambunctious behavior
inevitable with two young dogs together proved easy enough to
manage. When we finally decided to call it a morning, I asked
Ray to leash his dog and walked Rocky out on the bank to see
how he would respond to an opportunity to retrieve a bird on
his own.

While Rocky had enjoyed plenty of basic yard work with
dummies around the house and sniffed his share of the pheasants
I'd brought home that fall, he'd never held a bird in his mouth
much less retrieved one from the water. But motivated by the
general high spirits of the morning, I just couldn't resist the
opportunity to give him a chance. Expect nothing, I reminded
myself, and then I grabbed a warm mallard drake from the pile
and pitched it into the water at the edge of the decoys.

An encouraging Fetch! had barely left my mouth by the time
the little guy hit the water. I'd already chided myself for dropping
the bird so close to the decoys, but no matter. The puppy steamed
right past the distractions like a veteran, picked up the mallard
with a perfect firm-but-gentle grip across the back, and delivered
it to my outstretched hand, a feat made all the more remarkable
by the fact that the package looked bigger than its deliverer.

"How long have you been working him on ducks in the
water?" Ray asked.

"About thirty seconds," I replied.

"Well I'll be damned," Ray said, and I couldn't have put it
better myself.

Over the years I've listened to lots of discussion about how
much hunting experience is appropriate for a puppy during
the dog's first season and I'm not sure there is a right answer. I am

sure there is no one right answer, and that at the very least the
first season's hunting experience must be carefully tailored to the
dog. I also recognize that my approach may not be appropriate if
the goal is a field trial champion as opposed to a hunting companion. But for those of us who live to work our dogs in the field,
a dog's puppy season just offers too many opportunities to ignore.

All dogs develop according to different schedules and no
aspect of the training process emphasizes this variability like the
introduction to actual hunting conditions. Yard work allows the
trainer to control the variables, carefully introducing the dog to
new concepts in orderly fashion. On the other hand, even the
most carefully orchestrated hunting trip contains potential for the
unexpected, which makes hunting so exciting in the first place.
While I don't doubt that a day of confused shouting with lots of
distractions from other dogs and hunters can be a disaster for a
puppy, I've had too many wonderful experiences with young dogs
in the field to leave them all behind without giving them a chance
to share.

During their first year of life, individual retrievers mature at
variable rates that often correlate poorly with age according to
the calendar. Some prove more than ready to tag along at four or
five months while others really need to stay behind entirely until
their second season. Treating a dog in the second category as if it
belongs in the first only produces frustration for dog and handler
alike. The trick is to explore the possibilities gently and be honest about the dog's readiness for the field. As a general rule of
thumb, if the experience doesn't seem like fun for both you and
the dog, it's best to declare a time out.

On the other hand, some dogs appear so obviously precocious
that it would be a shame not to let them explore their potential

early. Years ago, Sky gave me a first season the likes of which I know I'll never see again. At the time, I ascribed his incredible early ability to my brilliance as a trainer but with the perspective of passing years I recognize that assessment as nonsense. The dog was simply an absolute natural and not even my own inexperience could compromise his ability. We lived in a game-rich, out-of-the-way corner of Montana at the time and Sky and I shared the kind of youthful enthusiasm that let us hunt more in one autumn than most dogs will hunt in their whole lives. I wouldn't have missed that season for anything.

The possibility of enjoying an experience like that must be balanced against the two potential drawbacks of taking a puppy hunting early: dampening the dog's enthusiasm by too much correction and allowing the youngster to develop bad habits that will return to haunt you later. Hard-mouthing birds illustrates both points. All pups like to chew. Let the dog get away with it in the field and you'll have all kinds of problems correcting this serious fault later, but get after the pup too hard and you'll both stop having fun, which defeats the whole purpose of the adventure.

Avoiding the hazards of too much, too soon can be summarized simply: don't set a puppy up to fail. Anticipate the pup's likely response to situations that commonly arise in the field. If it isn't likely to be favorable, take a break even if that means leaving the youngster behind. Hunting conditions are simply not the place to work out the basics. On the other hand, if the pup demonstrates enthusiasm and can get through a morning in a blind or take a turn through the cover without doing anything that requires much correction, why not?

After all, that's what Labs are all about. Just ask them.

The afternoon following our outing on the slough, I took Rocky down to the creek below our house. A warm sun had chased the last of the chill from the air and it felt like time to play, an attitude the dog evidently shared as he boiled out of the truck and set off through the snow by my side. Carrying one of the birds we'd shot that morning, I walked to the bank and studied the clear current gurgling past. After promising myself not to ask the dog for anything more than he wanted to give, I pitched the duck into a quiet backwater fifteen feet from shore and asked him to fetch.

I expected him to pick his way tentatively down the bank to the water, but he surprised me by hitting the creek in a geyser of spray and snagging the bird like a pro. After accepting the duck, I rolled up my waders and climbed down the bank myself, extending his range by three or four yards across the backwater with each retrieve. Finally, even though I sensed I should quit while we were both still ahead, I lobbed the duck into the current and watched Rocky swim it down without a hitch.

Two days later, I rose in the dark and headed back to the slough. Sonny had long since adjusted to the notion of retirement, but Jake stared in disbelief when I took the puppy along and left him behind. I felt badly for Jake, but after reviewing the week's events I'd decided Rocky had earned the right to go hunting without another dog along to distract him.

Reminding myself of the morning's priorities, I let the first set of birds circle over the brush on the far side of the slough without firing a shot. I knew exactly what we needed: one duck stone dead in the decoys, an absolutely obvious fall suitable for a retriever who was still, after all, very much a puppy. Then a single mallard drake appeared out of the sky like an answer to a prayer. As the bird descended over the top of the cottonwoods with wings cupped and air whistling through his primaries, I calculated the trajectory, rose at precisely the right moment... and flat out missed the chip shot. Twice.

Sonny would have given me one of his patented looks that says "I got up at 5 A.M. for that?" But Rocky didn't seem to care, which just goes to show how hunting with a young dog can provide unexpected sources of pleasure. I realized that I'd been so concerned about serving the bird up for the dog that I had forgotten the basic mechanics of wingshooting, and that the pup wasn't going to learn anything by watching me miss. When a set of four mallards swooped into the decoys a few minutes later, I picked out a drake and watched it crumple at the sound of the shot. I didn't even think about the second barrel, not with more pressing matters at hand.

Breaking the gun and resting it against a stump out of harm's way, I gave the dog the line and sent him. Undaunted by the slough's tenacious mud bottom, Rocky churned his way through the decoys, picked up the bird, and delivered it without ruffling a feather. And I have to admit that visions of another Skykomish danced through my head every step of the way.

As the season wound down, I knew we'd have to wait until the next to see how all that promise played out. But events already served to remind me that puppies are still puppies. Our next outing took place on the kind of blustery winter day that can really keep ducks moving. After standing beside the decoys for a quiet hour, waves of mallards began to appear above the horizon as the birds left the fields to return to the creek. When the first flock dropped in, I sent a drake mallard tumbling into the water right in front of us. But this time when I sent Rocky, he minced around on the bank and looked back over his shoulder as if I'd asked him to jump off a cliff. It took me a moment to recognize the problem: the dog was just plain cold. While the weather wouldn't have posed a problem for one of the older dogs, puppies are different. Just like kids, their high ratio of surface area to body mass leaves them more vulnerable to winter weather than adults, a fact I'd foolishly managed to overlook.

Fortunately, the dead bird lay in water shallow enough for me to negotiate in my waders without getting wet, and once I pitched the duck up the bank I set to work collecting the decoys even though flocks of mallards were filling the sky overhead. Leaving early goes against my grain, but I reminded myself that hunting with puppies is supposed to be fun for all, especially the dogs. And while there would be lots of days with ducks in the air, there was only going to be one Rocky.

Second Season

Welcome to the real world

The invitation came unsolicited, from a kindly ranch widow I've known for years. By reputation, she never let anyone hunt her place and to avoid putting her in an awkward position, I never asked. But then one afternoon as we concluded a few routine medical matters in the office, she suggested that Lori and I come out and hunt. I knew the area as prime bird cover, so she didn't have to ask twice.

My first good look at the terrain confirmed my initial enthusiasm. Long reaches of grass and cattails ran between golden rectangles of stubble, and in contrast to most of the neighboring places, the cover hadn't been grazed at all, leaving it in perfect condition to hold pheasants. As we pulled off the county road to park, a rooster erupted beside the vehicle and rocketed away down the draw. "Finally!" I said to Lori as I climbed out of the truck and walked around to release the dog from the kennel.

After his precocious performance the previous winter, Rocky and I spent a long, pleasant summer completing preparations for his first real season in the field. Given his enthusiasm and abundance of common sense, I entertained optimistic visions of the kind of autumn I'd last experienced with Sky nearly thirty years earlier, with birds galore and inspiring canine performances in both water and field. Unfortunately, nature had a series of cruel tricks up her sleeve.

While Rocky never faltered in his training, my concerns about the season ahead began in the spring, for reasons that had nothing to do with the dog. Months of exceptionally dry weather left much of our local bird cover looking as if it had been fertilized with Agent Orange. We finally received rain in early June—welcome news for the countryside and area farmers struggling to save their crops but poorly timed for vulnerable hatches of young upland birds. But I didn't appreciate the extent of the disaster until I hit the cover with my bow during September, also the beginning of sharptail season here in Montana. I've always been enthusiastic about working young dogs on sharptails and fully expected to watch Rocky spend the month translating all that yard work into real retrieves.

But there weren't any grouse: zero, zip, nada. Nowadays I usually do my sharptail scouting with my bow in my hand, but cover that ordinarily belched birds by the score remained stubbornly silent. I took the dog out several times anyway, but his nose only confirmed the obvious. I didn't want to burn him out on empty cover and I wouldn't have felt right about shooting many grouse if we'd found them, so I finally gave up, acknowledging that his introduction to upland game would have to wait until pheasant season.

So there we stood, facing unbroken miles of prime virgin pheasant cover. Since pheasants often re-nest successfully after a failed first hatch, I remained cautiously optimistic despite our dismal experience with the grouse in September. Because I was so anxious to work Rocky without distraction, I left Jake kenneled in the back of the truck, to his obvious displeasure. After chambering a pair of shells, we set off into what I hoped would be the legitimate beginning of bird season.

By the time we'd methodically covered a mile of cattails, however, my spirits had started to sink. We hadn't flushed a bird. Rocky remained tractable and reasonably enthusiastic, and I found it hard to fault him too strongly for failing to pound the heaviest cover, since I had yet to show him any reason to. As we circled back toward the road, he finally flushed a hen. I desperately wanted to drop the bird just to show him what the game was all about, but I couldn't find a way to make the bird's head turn green. When we finally reached the vehicle without firing a shot, I did my best to assure Jake he hadn't missed a thing.

The following morning, I set off for a nearby ranch that contains some of the most challenging cover I know: dense patches of willows laced with beaver workings that could hide moose as easily as pheasants. It's not the kind of place I'd ordinarily choose to hunt a young dog, but I knew that if we worked it hard enough we'd find some birds, and Rocky badly needed to taste some pheasant feathers before he decided he was meant to be a lap dog after all.

Such cover showcases the abilities of an aggressive, seasoned dog like Sonny in his prime, and as we waded into the brush I momentarily felt guilty about asking a boy to do a man's work. But Rocky behaved credibly for his level of experience, and after an hour of brambles and beaver-sharpened punji stakes he finally plowed into a clump of cattails and flushed a rooster. I think I would have retired for the season had I missed that long-awaited bird, but at the shotgun's report the rooster crumpled and fell near the edge of a nearby field, leaving the dog with a relatively easy retrieve.

While he had no difficulty recovering the bird, which fortunately fell stone-dead, he quickly forgot all the yard-training we'd done over the summer and spat the rooster out prematurely rather than delivering it to hand… hardly an uncommon flaw in a youngster no matter what the dog's previous level of training. Anxious to divorce celebration of his accomplishment from correction of the fault, I praised him, broke the gun, and sat down at the edge of the grass. Five minutes later, we repeated the basic drills we'd practiced on pigeons all summer, and by the time we headed back into the cover again, he seemed to have absorbed the lesson.

After several more pheasant hunts that involved a lot more hunting than shooting, I felt reasonably satisfied with Rocky's performance. His only real weakness seemed to be lack of enthusiasm for heavy cover which, given the paucity of birds, I found easy enough to understand. Somehow, I needed to teach him that on pheasant hunts he belonged in the brush and not at my side. Then one morning I decided to run him with Jake, Rocky's total opposite in terms of personality. Assertive to a fault, Jake has never been a particularly pleasant dog to work with, but he has always hit the cover with determination. With the older dog showing the way, Rocky seemed far more eager to explore the thick brush along the creek bottom we hunted that day, and the fact that we actually managed to kill a few roosters helped reinforce the lesson. I'm not always enthusiastic about working youngsters with other dogs because of the potential for confusion. But difficult circumstances require imaginative approaches and rules are made to be broken.

I admit that I'm spoiled. I live in an area that supports plenty of wild birds and I know the country well. Ordinarily, the difference between a good pheasant year and a poor one means walk-

ing one hour to shoot a limit instead of three. But in thirty years on the prairie, I'd never seen a season quite as desperate as this one. It's not that I'm lazy. I still enjoy testing my legs against the contour lines of a steep coulee, and to tell the truth I usually enjoy those three-hour limits more than the easy ones. But long hikes with no birds didn't seem to be teaching Rocky much about the game, and after a few more lackluster hunts, I decided to go bowhunting and wait for the ducks.

Once again, nature proved a fickle mistress. Northern mallards usually begin to arrive around my home in late October, but unseasonably warm weather left me hunting in shirtsleeves long after I've usually donned woolens. The creeks and sloughs around town remained barren and I began to wonder if I'd ever manage to salvage Rocky's first real season.

Winter finally arrived the weekend after Thanksgiving. As the mercury plummeted and snow swirled down from the sky, ice enclosed the ponds, the sound of geese filled the air overhead at last and I began to notice plump mallards crowded into the open bends along the creek as I drove to work. Finally, it felt like time to take Rocky hunting again.

We rose early and headed for a favorite spring fed slough beneath low overcast skies. The thermometer had crept above the freezing level overnight, which concerned me a little since our late season ducks disperse rapidly whenever local ponds begin to open up. Lori, on the other hand, couldn't have been happier, since she'll trade a few birds for warm feet any day. My concerns proved groundless, for as soon as we finished untangling the decoy lines and cast out a few blocks, the sound of setting wings tore through the air overhead.

I barely had time to scramble back to shore and load my shotgun. With Lori managing the dog, I isolated a plump drake from the settling flock and reminded myself what Rocky really needed: a dead mallard hitting the water right in front of him. But I wound up dropping the bird in a tangle of cattails on the far side of the slough with my second barrel. "I thought you said you were going to give him nothing but easy ones," Lori reminded me as Rocky hit the water.

"No comment," I replied. But the dog's work proved sounder than my own, and a few minutes later my shooting lapse became forgotten history as we celebrated Rocky's return with the neatly delivered bird.

That morning, the slough never offered the furious shooting we often experience there during sub-zero weather, but enough birds dropped in over the next two hours to let me atone for my early miss and give Rocky a true taste of waterfowling. His enthusiastic and generally encouraging performance reminded me of several caveats that apply to any young dog's introduction

to new hunting situations:
Doubles are easier to keep track
of on the lawn than from a duck
blind. The places we hunt offer a
wide range of distractions.
Marking long falls requires experience to master. Mud is meant
to be shared with friends.

But by the time we unloaded
and began to pick up the decoys,
we'd fulfilled the most important
criterion for success on any such
an outing: Rocky had enjoyed himself and so had we.

I've always entertained ambivalent feelings about report cards.
Even as a kid, I recognized the fundamental absurdity of reduc-
ing months' worth of study to a letter or number. And there
always seemed to be something better to do than jump through
the conventional hoops required to make those letters and numbers what they were supposed to be. But I also learned at an
early age that good report cards reliably translated into opportunities to go hunting with my father, even at the occasional
expense of school. And so I made my own pact with the devil,
and as such pacts go, that was surely one of my more harmless.

First a word of explanation in Rocky's defense. I've never
endorsed the modern tendency toward grade inflation, which
allows anyone who shows up a B and those who actually pretend
to do anything A's. Call me old fashioned, but C still means what
it once did: average.

And now—with my apologies—it's your turn, Rocky, for the
whole world to see.

Name: West Wind's Rocket

Grade: First

Teacher: Thomas

Upland Game: B-

       Strengths: Obedient, gentle mouth.

       Weaknesses: Uncertain nose, tentative in heavy cover.

Waterfowl: A-

       Strengths: Enthusiasm for water, good blind manners.

       Weaknesses: Uncertain marking ability, strays off task.

Comments: A pleasure to have in class. Relates well to teachers and peers. Good study habits. Needs to show more initiative in order to realize full potential. Good luck in the second grade!

Amen.

Road Trip!

Hunting beyond the next horizon

With Christmas and New Year a matter of record, rural Montana's potential for mid-winter monotony finally began to rear its ugly head. Dull brown prairie stretched away endlessly beneath dull gray skies, defying even the most ambitious photographer inspiring light. Long, cold nights enveloped the countryside, inducing an acute urge to join the local bears in hibernation. Even old friends grew testy and none of the dogs seemed interested in leaving the hearth. The last few weeks of waterfowl season kept my growing despair in check for a while, since a limit of greenheads can make almost any circumstances endurable. But then duck season closed, and the absence of snow denied me even the quirky pleasure of chasing mountain lions. The hour for desperate measures rolled around at last, and the solution, as John Belushi and company concluded in Animal House, proved simple. Road trip!

The value of a good road trip depends upon the need to escape one's current circumstances as much as what lies ahead. But last January, we enjoyed especially attractive options. Seattle's restaurants and theaters lay one long day's drive to the west, and I hadn't seen my parents since their annual visit during pheasant season. More to the point, my father maintains a principal interest in a Columbia Basin ranch managed predominantly for waterfowl, and Washington's duck season was still open.

Furthermore, we enjoy a standing invitation to visit our old friends Joe and Karen Kelly outside Wenatchee, where quail and chukar seasons were still open as well. Talk about no-brainers. Work—our usual regrettable antidote for winter tedium—could wait a little longer.

Other than a road, the only absolute requirement for a successful road trip is a vehicle, which doesn't have to be much. Over the years, I've made some of my most memorable forays in cars and trucks barely capable of running, let alone offering any creature comforts. But circumstances have changed a bit since my student days, and after a few quick phone calls to family and friends we loaded Lori's Navigator with all the items a devoted son should carry on a visit to Mom and Dad: shotgun, shells, waders, foul weather gear and, finally, Rocky.

Rocky was already experienced enough to feel the excitement in the air. He's appreciated what it means to board a vehicle carrying gun cases ever since he was a puppy. With his travel kennel securely nestled beneath a small mountain of gear, he made one final tour about the rig and jumped the tailgate enthusiastically, and with that, we hit the road.

Not a moment too soon, in my opinion.

Dawn arrived in slow motion the following day as the sun struggled feebly against an industrial strength fog layer shrouding the mighty Columbia. In a sense, I regretted the gloom, since I hadn't hunted the property for some time and eagerly awaited my first good look at the place after an absence of several years. But the ears nearly completed a picture the eyes could not as a rich chorus of duck talk rose to a crescendo in the mist around the blind. Then wings began to whistle overhead and dark silhouettes splashed into the decoys, sending gentle shudders across the glassy surface of the pond. Overall, the spectacle seemed designed to remind me how much I miss the grand pageantry of duck hunting at its finest.

Actually, Lori and I don't live in an area noted for its waterfowl. Our home county boasts an abundance of upland birds, big game and trout, but situated in dry terrain on the cusp between the Central and Pacific Flyways, it just doesn't support a lot of ducks. I can always scrounge up a duck dinner with sufficient effort and the late season mallard hunting can be spectacular, but I still miss the Big Show: broad wetlands, enough birds overhead to require an air traffic controller, variety sufficient to make quick identification on the wing a necessary skill. I'll trade a quick limit of greenheads for that kind of duck hunting any day.

As the minute hands on our coordinated watches crept toward legal shooting light, I began to call out the names of species as ducks appeared overhead just to celebrate the joy all that variety offered. "Pintails!" I cried as a pair of sprig rocketed past the blocks. "Remember them," I reminded Lori. "Pintail season closed last week in the Pacific flyway."

"How do you know they're pintails?" she asked.

"Because they look like pintails," I replied. Fortunately for the sake of marital accord, my father announced the official arrival of shooting light just then, and when a mallard drake set its wings overhead moments later he dropped it just beyond the decoys.

For the next three hours, the pace of the shooting somehow managed to remain just right. Any faster and it would have been over too soon, but we enjoyed the sight and sound of birds overhead almost without interruption. Since my folks prefer to shoot and eat mallards and I hadn't enjoyed an opportunity at anything else for months, I left the greenheads to them while I toyed with the rest like an inquisitive diner at a table full of exotic gourmet delights. By the end of the morning, a half-dozen species of ducks lay on the bench beside me, including a drake woodie I planned to take to the taxidermist, and I'd let more pintails flare overhead than I'd seen in two seasons at home.

Rocky took home a mixed report card for the day. Given the distractions of a fully occupied blind and unfamiliar circumstances, matters certainly could have turned out worse. Despite the close quarters and general hubbub, his blind manners and overall deportment rated his usual A, as did his gentle mouth. The tightly constructed blind made marking difficult, but he performed satisfactorily. As for handling, well... Thomas' Law does state that all dogs must demonstrate some element of ineptitude in the presence of respected witnesses. Let's just say it became clear that he needed to learn to translate some of the training he'd mastered in the yard into actual hunting conditions in the field, hardly an uncommon lapse in a youngster. At any rate, his performance left us with some clear guidelines for the work we needed to do over the winter.

And there was certainly plenty of winter waiting for us back home.

Those of us who long to hunt new and distant country but can't imagine doing so without our own dogs face difficult choices these days. Thanks to misguided—or deliberate, if you choose—efforts by various animal "welfare" groups, traveling by air with dogs has become unbelievably (and unnecessarily) complicated and expensive. Back when I lived in Alaska, Sky and I flew back to Montana every fall with nary a glitch at little if any

extra cost. Those days are over now, making a good old-fashioned road trip an increasingly attractive option. With a little time, the right attitude and sufficient planning, getting there can be a relatively stress-free process if not quite half the fun.

The easiest mistake in planning long road trips with dogs is the assumption they will behave just as they do at home. In fact, trained dogs are creatures of habit, and new environments and distractions can always produce unexpected behavior. Respect Murphy's Law and plan ahead.

The first equipment requirement is an adequate kennel, to provide control during transport and comfortable quarters. Around home, I carry my dogs in a huge, solidly built wooden dog box, but that arrangement is too ponderous and space-consuming for real road travel. Lightweight, airline-style kennels are a far more convenient option.

Leashes are equally important, no matter how well trained the dog. Even steady dogs can bolt unpredictably after periods of confinement in a kennel, especially in strange surroundings. On the road, those jaunts may take place near a busy highway with disastrous consequences. I always pack extra leashes, and to remind myself of their importance I leave one clipped on the front of the kennel where I can't miss it.

Traveling dogs generally have no trouble eating at slightly irregular intervals, but water can be more problematic. In hot weather, it's imperative to offer dogs water regularly since a kenneled dog has even less control over the ambient temperature than the vehicle's driver, who can at least enjoy a blast of fresh air from the window periodically. I always carry a 5-gallon can so I can provide water to the dog at every rest stop. Water dishes splash and spill on the road, which is why I favor the square, splash-resistant model offered by Dunn's.

Motels and campgrounds demonstrate varying attitudes toward dogs, ranging from "let 'em sleep on the bed" to "none allowed—no exceptions". Whenever possible, check these matters out in advance. When in doubt, remember the Golden Rule and respect the sensibilities of your temporary neighbors. Walk dogs in out of the way locations rather than the middle of the motel parking lot. Even polite dogs may bark in strange locations, which is why I carry a bark collar when I travel (although I forgot it this time, to my folks' temporary consternation when we reached their house). If nothing else, these courtesies will make it easier for the next hunter enjoying a road trip with his or her canine best friends.

Restaurants and theaters… Did I really say that? Fortunately, the big city didn't last long and after two days of pleasant family affairs we loaded up again and headed back over the Cascades to chukar country.

Although I hadn't hunted chukar seriously in several years, I grew up chasing these elusive partridge through eastern Washington's rugged breaks and had grown to miss the challenge of the terrain they inhabit and the great sweeping arcs they transcribe on the wing when flushed from the rocks. But as Joe, Lori and I unloaded our gear at the bottom of the first coulee and started up the grade, something felt different, as if I'd landed on a planet with a gravitational field stronger than Earth's. After a long, rugged autumn that included extended bowhunts for mountain goat, sheep and lion, I should have been in shape for anything. But no doubt about it: in the decade since I'd last hunted these hills, some mysterious force had made them steeper.

Some might question the utility of a flushing dog in the pursuit of chukar, and no doubt a wide-ranging retriever may hurt more than help. But I worked Rocky tightly at heel and he accepted the constraint gladly, although it's hard to say whether his manners owed more to training or the terrain. Our intention was to locate and flush a covey of birds and then use Rocky and Joe's dog to root out tight sitting singles. At least that was the plan.

Our first sweep up the draw yielded a covey of quail on Joe's side, and I stood and watched while he dropped four with as many shots. We'd climbed steadily into rougher, rockier terrain by the time I cut the first chukar tracks in the powdery snow. The trail looked fresh and with Rocky at heel, I followed the sign all the way to the crest of a ridge overlooking the broad Columbia far below. Suddenly, the tracks disappeared where the covey had taken flight, an obstacle I've never had to face when tracking deer or cougar.

Feeling thoroughly defeated, I sat down on a rock to catch my breath and plot my exit from the cliffs. I'd lost track of Joe and Lori, and as I turned around to look for them, the familiar ping!

of a chukar's alarm call rose above the sigh of the breeze. Wings locked, a single swung out away from the rocks and arced across the vast expanse of open air in front of me. I scrambled for my shotgun, drove the muzzle far in front of the accelerating bird, and watched with immense satisfaction is it crumpled at the sound of the shot.

But we weren't eating chukar yet. Because of the cliff's steep pitch and the speeding bird's momentum, it hit the ground a good two hundred yards below me. But Rocky had this fall locked in his radar, and after a wild descent through terrain better suited to mountain goats than ordinary feathered game, he ran the bird down and delivered it flawlessly, affording the first good look at a chukar I'd enjoyed in years.

The hills may have grown steeper, but I could still negotiate them. The country I'd grown up in may have become crowded, but the birds were still there, protected from hunting pressure by the severity of their habitat. Sometimes, it seems, the best road trips are those that lead you home.

Special Delivery

Some game birds demand more of dogs than others

As the dull winter sunrise crept slowly over the windswept plains, we listened to the sound of the geese on the water below us swell to a cacophony. It takes a lot of noise to fill an entire river valley, but the vast flocks of northern birds eventually brought the racket to deafening levels. Finally, geese began to lift off from patches of open water between leads of ice and circle to gain elevation as they headed for the stubble fields behind us. At this point, an unruly dog might have spoiled everything, but Rocky sat patiently at my side, studying the distant flights as they began to clear the level of the horizon. I couldn't remember seeing a young dog more ready to meet his first goose.

The first few flocks sailed past well out of range. Then a group of a dozen birds neatly split the distance between my position and Ray's fifty yards down the line. He deferred to me, I deferred to him, and the geese glided by none the wiser. "Somebody better start shooting!" I called out, and when the next set flew overhead I rose and followed my own advice.

Pass shooting geese can be a challenging game. Over decoys, I'll often ignore the easiest bird, leaving it for the back half of a hypothetical double (admittedly with occasional regrets.) But at these ranges, I was concentrating on one bird at a time when the next flight appeared overhead. When the lowest goose shuddered at my first shot, I hit it again for good measure and watched with immense satisfaction as it tumbled out of the sky and hit the

ground at the base of the steep bank below us while two more
shots rang out from Ray's direction. When he began working his
own dog, I broke cover and sent Rocky down the hill.

Steep terrain made the fall difficult to mark, but Rocky took
the line crisply and soon disappeared into a dense clump of brush
while I watched Ray's young Chessie run down his long cripple.
When Rocky didn't emerge for some time, I surmised that the
bird might have lodged in branches too high for him to reach
and worked my way down the bank to lend a hand. In fact, the
dead goose had reached the ground and Rocky had located it
deep in the brush. But he was sitting next to the huge greater
Canada with an expression that plainly declared, "I don't know
what that is, but it ain't in my job description!"

Although still young, Rocky was hardly inexperienced. He'd
spent plenty of time in the field, and had demonstrated excellent
mouth manners on a wide variety of waterfowl and upland game.
While I'd certainly seen young dogs balk at geese before, his refusal
caught me off guard, since he'd performed so well in such a variety
of hunting situations earlier. Despite his obvious lack of enthusiasm for the big bundle of feathers beside him, I still didn't anticipate more than a moment's difficulty convincing him that geese
were basically just big mallards and should be treated accordingly.

Extracting bird and dog from the brambles, I made Rocky sit
and offered him the goose with the command to fetch. Nothing
doing. Ear pressure resulted in an open mouth and tentative
acceptance of the goose, but he refused to hold. "Birds overhead!"
I heard Ray cry from the top of the hill, and I looked up to see
geese flaring out of range at the sight of our impromptu training
session. Ray and I have always demonstrated great tolerance
toward one another's young dogs, but it certainly wasn't his fault
that Rocky had suddenly forgotten his basics. Somewhat reluc-

tantly, I threw the goose over my shoulder and started to climb
back up the hill with the dog at heel. Back at my makeshift
blind, I tied Rocky to his leash and let Ray's dog handle the rest
of the retrieving chores. Even two more hours of challenging but
steady shooting couldn't distract me from the realization that
some serious work awaited us back home.

Virtually all retrievers begin their careers fetching some artificial
substitute for the real thing. No wonder; dummies are cheap, convenient and perfectly adequate for teaching the basics. Live birds,
on the other hand, are a hassle at best and an expensive, messy
hassle the rest of the time. Hopefully, most dogs trained for the
field will enjoy at least a brief introduction to shackled pigeons
before opening day, but even then it pays to recognize an important point, especially when training a truly versatile working
retriever: not all birds are created equal, and no one appreciates the
differences like the dogs that have to hold them in their mouths.

Fortunately, most common game species—upland birds and
waterfowl alike—don't cause a lot of problems for trained retrievers, even on their first introduction. I've seldom if ever had well-
started dogs balk at their first encounter with grouse or
partridge. The same holds true for ducks, at least partly because
they're usually hunted in cooler weather and often fall in the
water, where a young dog is less likely to realize he's fetching
something other than a dummy until the retrieve is complete.
But all these species share several important characteristics that
make them easy for young dogs to retrieve: they are about the
size of a retriever's mouth, their feathers are compact and don't
dislodge easily, and they're seldom aggressive.

Here in my part of the world, I like to introduce my dogs to
upland game with sharptails, for all the reasons just mentioned. It
doesn't hurt that sharptail season starts early, but they're also a lot

easier for young dogs to manage than two other early season species discussed below. After a few weeks of sharptails, we usually move on to teal over decoys and a few jump-shooting trips for whatever puddle ducks happen to be around. Then—and only then—if all is going well, it's time to move on to more difficult game.

Doves are one important example. A lot of dogs don't like fetching doves, and despite the appeal of starting the season with a fast and furious dove shoot, I usually leave the retrieving chores to one of the older dogs and wait until the youngster in the kennel has had a successful season under his belt before inviting him along. Doves have loose plumage and young dogs don't appreciate feathers sticking to their tongues. Equally important, dove hunting often takes place in very hot weather, and it's hard to pant holding a bird in your mouth. When I do take a young dog on his first dove hunt, I carry plenty of water in the vehicle, try to set up near a water source so the dog can cool down easily, and minimize the inevitable running around all enthusiastic dogs like to engage in, especially on the first hunt of the year. An overheated dog and a mouth full of dove feathers do not make a good combination, especially for a youngster.

The only reason sage hens aren't a problem for more retrievers is that not very many get to hunt them. Here in Montana, sage grouse and sharptail seasons open at the same time, but, as with doves, I prefer to leave young dogs behind on sage hen hunts until they've had a bit of experience. Probably because of a combination of the birds' size and pungency, dogs often balk the first time they encounter dead sage hens, and I prefer them to have mastered the basics on other species first.

Pheasants can cause problems for a young dog for very different reasons. In contrast to the species mentioned earlier, wounded pheasants like to run… and occasionally fight back. Running crip-

ples can bring out a young dog's pr[...] to hard-mouthing. At the first sign [...] take a break and go back to the bas[...] trolled conditions, even if that mea[...] the other hand, a dog that receives [...] attempt to retrieve a pheasant may [...] one for some time. Even after train[...] warming up on easier game, all dog[...] the challenge of their own first wild [...] which no training regimen can tota[...] tions will help. In the beginning, h[...] understand these things, so you wo[...] have to interrupt the hunt for the b[...] vehicle with a second dog in reserve [...] if need be. And try to make sure th[...]

And then there are geese… W[...] night, I cleaned three birds f[...] house and left the fourth hanging i[...] The following morning, I rose early [...] ing session I hoped would correct [...] the last weekend of the season. No [...] ferent approaches to this problem, [...] considerable leeway in their initial [...] big honker, after all, is quite a load, [...] learn how to handle it in stepwise f[...]

I began by throwing a few dum[...] begin the session on a positive note [...] command. Then I substituted a go[...] evening for the dummy. Five minu[...] fortable with the smell and taste of [...]

Bulk w[...]
dummies [...]
whole me[...]
smell, this [...]
had no tr[...]
down and [...]
practiced [...]
hold the b[...]

I wante[...]
the Real [...]
pheasants [...]
Our next [...]
same weig[...]
handle th[...]

I place[...]
worry abo[...]
command [...]
tackled th[...]
first goose [...]
the neck. [...]
drop with [...]
perfectly [...]
and let R[...]

The ch[...]
a known s[...]
but steadi[...]
reinforce [...]
declare vi[...]

Then [...]
Rocky an[...]

LIFE WITH LABS

We've already explored the Labrador retriever's remarkable hunting talents, both as water dog and flushing retriever in upland cover. Appropriately enough, since hunting brings out the heart of a Lab and the breed's versatility provides one of the central themes driving this text. But this collection presents another thesis as well. Each of the Labs that enrich our lives represents a unique personality reflecting such admirable characteristics as loyalty, enthusiasm, devotion and courage, and the dogs' importance to us derives from their role as companions and family members as much as from their performance in the field.

Back when I was a kid, my father trained pointers, some of which we ran in field trials. It didn't take us long to realize that field trial standards had little if anything to do with the qualities we sought in our dogs when we hunted grouse and woodcock in thick cover. Retriever trials generally set standards far more appropriate to hunting situations, at least as they apply to waterfowling. But those standards don't always correlate perfectly with optimal performance on opening day, especially in the pursuit of upland game.

Retriever training books tend to be written by people who win field trials. Fair enough; professional trainers certainly know more about the subject than I ever will. But with all due respect, this process tends to reduce dogs and their handling to vectors and choreography. Nothing wrong with that to the extent of the purpose it serves, but losing track of the dogs as individuals shortchanges all involved. The rewards Labs have provided me over the years just depend on so much more.

And so, a potpourri to fill in some of the blanks between flushes and retrieves, from sentiment to observations around the house and a tribute to a delightfully flawed favorite. By the time we're through, I hope you'll understand a little more about my passion for Labs and why I'd give my kingdom—if I had one— for their company.

The Ice Fog

When it comes to old dogs, decisions sometimes prove as murky as the weather.

I hated to admit it, but I felt cold as soon as we left the truck. Since I hail from central Montana, I'm supposed to be accustomed to hunting waterfowl under challenging conditions, but Alberta in November knows how to stretch my tolerance to the limits. I'd timed my visit to coincide with the whitetail rut, but my old friend Jeff Lander likes to hunt ducks just as much as I do and after several days of frustration courtesy of the area's wary bucks we'd traded bows for shotguns. Days of frigid weather had locked most of the local ponds in ice and sent lots of waterfowl winging south, but Jeff knows the area intimately and he'd found open water despite the chill. With his enthusiastic scouting report still ringing in my ears, I knew we were in for a good shoot… provided we could persevere long enough to enjoy it.

Back home, sub-zero waterfowling usually takes place under clear skies and the sparkling beauty of a bright winter landscape can make up for a lot of physical discomfort. But for the past three days, a dense layer of ice fog had shrouded the Edmonton area, obscuring the sun and permeating our heavy woolens with bone-chilling cold. As we lugged our decoy bags through the snow, mist rose from the open surface of the spring-fed pond and condensed immediately in the chill, creating an atmosphere that felt more like whipped cream than air. But somewhere overhead, wing beats whistled through the gloom to remind us why we had entered this eerie boreal version of purgatory.

Our friend Sonny Schierl and his young lab Logan accompanied us that morning. A young couple who had not yet got around to having kids of their own, Sonny and his wife Kim plainly felt happy to let Logan occupy that niche in their family. Charmingly spoiled, Logan reminded me of my own first yellow Lab—Bogey—back when I too lacked two-legged children to compete with dogs for my attention. An obvious character, Logan provided non-stop comic relief around camp, but his sudden intensity at the sight of the shotguns as we loaded the truck that morning established that beneath his antics lay the soul of a hunter.

Whitney, Jeff's ancient female chocolate Lab, formed the second half of the canine team. Jeff and I had communicated extensively about her prior to my arrival. She had experienced a series of health problems earlier in the fall, and Jeff's vet had openly discussed putting her down. Although three decades of medical practice have given me more experience than most with difficult end-of-life decisions, I still felt awkward when Jeff called and asked my opinion. I hadn't seen Whitney in two seasons, and my recent experiences with Sonny, my own old-timer, left me acutely aware of the speed with which the dogs we love can age.

Since Whitney didn't appear to be in any immediate distress, Jeff elected to temporize pending my arrival. I emphasized in advance that I am not a veterinarian and that whatever advice I had to offer would be based primarily on friendship and experience rather than medical judgment. Nonetheless, I made no effort to conceal my pleasant surprise when I first saw the dog again. The old girl looked dignified and comfortable, and appeared to have little difficulty getting around camp. Furthermore, she offered the kind of warm, sloppy greeting that made it clear she remembered me even after a two-year absence. Perhaps all patients should lick their doctors' faces more often.

For days we'd danced around the issue of whether or not to invite Whitney to go hunting. For better or worse, she pretty much solved the problem for us. When we threw the last of the decoys into the back of the rig and watched Logan bounce onto the tailgate, Whitney appeared wearing a wounded look that announced her intention to curse us all for life if we left her behind. As I bent down to boost her into the truck, she suddenly gave a mighty lunge. Her head caught me on the point of my chin with an impact that sent me to my knees in the snow. "Looks like she wants to go," I finally mumbled to Jeff, reminding myself that a few loose teeth seemed a small price to pay for the privilege of taking an old dog hunting.

By the time we reached the waterline, an intermittent breeze had started to open tantalizing gaps in the fog layer. Whenever the air cleared, we could see vortices of ducks circling nearby fields only to lose sight of them once more as the wind faltered and the fog coalesced. Frozen digits fumbling, we set to work on the decoys. Since Sonny and I were wearing waders, we climbed down the bank and into the water while Jeff wrestled with the inevitable mess of tangled lines inside the decoy bags. Logan, of course, proved eager to help while Whitney won the IQ contest by curling up on my heavy coat and going to sleep on top of the snow.

Spread placed at last, we each beat out a nest in a convenient swath of cattails and settled in to wait. Whitney looked so serene atop my coat that I didn't have the heart to fight her for it. For the time being, my wool shirt and vest kept the chill at bay although I wasn't sure my compassion for an old dog would survive my first serious shivering attack. Then the ice fog closed overhead again, leaving us nothing to do but stare at the amorphous sea of gray in search of ducks.

Finally I heard the unmistakable whistle of a goldeneye's wings approaching through the soup and shifted my feet into shooting position. The sound grew louder and louder as if someone were controlling it with a rheostat, but my eyes detected nothing. Suddenly the bird appeared, an abstract bundle of black and white silhouetted against the fog, devoid of any figure-ground relationship. I brought the borrowed automatic to my shoulder, drove it through the bird's outline, and slapped the trigger. To my surprise, the duck shuddered and collapsed, hitting the water with a distinctly audible plop only to be swallowed immediately by the fog.

"Nice shot!" someone offered encouragingly from the frozen cattails.

"If you say so," I replied, for the whole experience felt so detached and dreamy I couldn't remember much about it.

Then Jeff appeared beside me with Whitney at heel. "What do you think?" he asked.

I sensed that Jeff really wanted to see Whitney make one last retrieve even though he felt ambivalent about sending her. "Let's let the dog decide," I replied, a suggestion that had already become a fait accompli. Together, we watched Whitney waddle down the bank and splash into the water before she disappeared in the gloom. Moments later, she paddled her way back to shore with the bird in her mouth and I knew that somehow we had made all the right decisions. While Jeff offered praise and allowed her a gentle romp with the bird, I took advantage of the distraction to exchange two empty decoy bags for the coat she'd occupied previously. If she ever noticed this sleight of hand, she remained too polite to comment.

For the next two hours we enjoyed some of the spookiest duck shooting imaginable. I choose the word shooting, as opposed to hunting, deliberately. There happened to be a lot of ducks in the area and we happened to have picked a strategically located point to set up. Beyond these considerations, finding ourselves within range of waterfowl largely proved a passive affair, requiring us to do little but swing and fire whenever birds materialized from the fog. We quickly recognized that the ducks couldn't see the decoys in the mist. So we did a lot of calling, not the artful seduction one might offer a flock of mallards working a distant line of marsh but the loud, undisciplined bleating hunters lapse into when they can't think of anything better to do. How effective were those efforts? Beats me; I only know we shot plenty of ducks.

The shooting itself felt just plain weird. We couldn't see the birds coming but they couldn't see us either, so we simply lounged around in the snow, concentrated on the sound of wings and picked off ducks as they broke briefly through the ceiling. Oddly enough, we didn't miss many and to our even greater satisfaction we didn't lose a single fallen bird.

Credit for the latter accomplishment belongs to Logan. With Whitney's ritual retrieve out of the way, she snoozed the rest of the morning away while Logan fetched his heart out. He didn't do anything very sophisticated but the circumstances called for enthusiasm more than finesse and he showed us plenty.

When our fingers finally grew numb and we could no longer stomp around in the snow hard enough to keep our feet warm, we looked at one another and admitted we'd had enough. Setting decoys out on a bitter cold morning may be a miserable experience, but it's nothing compared to picking them up again when the shooting's done. By the time we started back to the truck burdened down by ducks as well as gear, only Logan seemed reluctant to quit a few birds shy of our limit, not that any of us expected anything else from a two-year old Labrador retriever.

As we trudged along through the snow, I considered the likelihood that we had all just witnessed Whitney's last retrieve. When it comes to managing hunting dogs at the end of their careers, there are probably no right answers and certainly no easy ones. Making an old campaigner do something it doesn't want to do may verge on cruelty, but denying one an opportunity it badly wants to enjoy may be even worse. Somehow, I suspected we'd found a fair compromise that morning somewhere inside the confounding layer of fog. Huffing along happily at Jeff's side, Whitney certainly seemed to think so, and I suppose that's the vote that counts most.

Just as we reached the truck, the sky began to clear overhead, and the sun broke through for the first time in days.

Four for the Books

Highlight films for upland retrievers

Pheasant season closed here in Montana this weekend. Bird numbers were down thanks to a wet spring and for two months we earned what we killed. True to form, on the last Sunday of the season Lori, Ray Stalmaster and I took the dogs out and walked all day for four roosters, which happened to be all the birds we shot at and just about all we saw. The retrieves proved utterly routine, and by the time we loaded back up to begin the drive home I couldn't even remember just which dog had fetched what.

Competent dogs—let alone great ones—have a way of doing that to you. Once past the gee-whiz stage of a young dog's first productive season, it's easy to start taking routine plays for granted, and that's a shame for all concerned. One way to rekindle the appreciation of a solid, workman-like retriever's performance is to go shoot a few birds without one, and we'll discuss that subject in a later chapter. Another is to remember days when difficult circumstances reminded you what the dog was capable of all along.

Retriever enthusiasts usually associate heroic retrieves with waterfowl, appropriately enough. There's something about breaking waves and big water that immediately suggests the epic. But upland dogs make heart-stopping retrieves as well, and during the long drive home from that final pheasant hunt of the year, we reviewed some of our all-time favorites. Interestingly, none reflects a lot of technical brilliance or the kind of style that wins field trials, although each remains instructive in its own way. And all confirm the enduring value of the versatile retriever even when the quarry is something other than ducks or geese.

A Thousand Vertical Feet

A pointing dog man at heart, my father was always ready to settle for the way his shorthairs and Brittanies fetched downed game until he met Skykomish, my first really great Lab. I still remember the retrieve that opened his eyes to the breed's possibilities.

I had traveled back to my parents' home in Washington for Christmas when Dad and I decided to drive across the mountains and hunt chukar with friends for a day. We were a lot younger then and the cliffs that rose above the Columbia north of Wenatchee failed to intimidate us, although we probably should have known better. Sky had never seen a chukar before, but given his level of youthful enthusiasm at the time I didn't anticipate much problem with the introduction. After a long traverse across a rocky side hill above the cliffs, we finally encountered a covey of birds. Chukar being chukar, they didn't offer much of a shot. I missed, but my father managed to drop one bird on the initial rise. The birds had flushed out away from the steep pitch of the hill, and by the time the bird finished falling it looked as if it had landed half a mile below us.

"Now what?" Dad asked.

"Beats me," I replied with a shrug, because the terrain between our position and the area of the fall looked impossible to cross without technical climbing gear. But I had reckoned without Sky.

As we stood and studied the jumbled talus below, Sky appeared bounding downward through the rocks, agile as a mountain goat. I'm still not sure how he managed to mark the fall, but as we watched in disbelief, he scooped up the bird and set off back uphill in our direction. In contrast to humans, dogs generally find it easier to go downhill than up in difficult terrain, and for a moment I thought we might have to go all the way back to the truck and drive to the base of the hill to retrieve the retriever. But he eventually managed to reach a position from which I could grab his collar and haul him upward—with the bird cradled gently but firmly in his mouth.

It was the kind of retrieve that can make anyone a believer. Just ask my Dad.

THE AIRBORNE CHESSIE

While Labs remain the stars of this volume, it only seems fair to offer a tip of the hat to another version of the theme: the Chesapeake Bay retriever. For years, Ray Stalmaster hunted with a diffident chocolate-colored Chessie named Lester. The dog had his share of faults, and I don't think Ray himself would be offended by the suggestion that this chapter doesn't contain space enough to list them all. But Lester still spent a useful life in service, and he demonstrated more flair for dramatic leaps and water entries than any dog I've ever seen.

One October afternoon late in Lester's derby year found us hunting pheasants along a steeply eroded creek bottom just south of the Missouri Breaks. That country contains a lot of up and down, and the high banks on the outside of each bend in the creek we were hunting along rose far above the bottom. The terrain made a lot of work for hunters and dogs alike, but the thick

cover contained plenty of birds and the pace of the shooting
more than made up for the steep going and the sting of the wild
rose thorns. On the last rise of the day, a rooster flushed at the
edge of my range, shuddered at the shot, and sailed over the edge
of one of these high banks and out of sight. As Ray and I
watched in disbelief, Lester tore off after the bird, and when he
reached the end of the terra firma he simply kept going although
neither of us could imagine how.

   As we hustled our way to the edge of the bank to begin the
search for the body, Lester emerged from the cover below...
alive, covered with mud, and carrying the pheasant. The lay of
the land made it apparent that he had bailed off the cliff in full
stride from precipitous height. Fortunately, his momentum had
carried him all the way to the creek where the water cushioned
the impact of his fall. When he delivered the bird to Ray's outstretched hand, he seemed entirely nonchalant about his air-

easier for young dogs to manage than two other early season species discussed below. After a few weeks of sharptails, we usually move on to teal over decoys and a few jump-shooting trips for whatever puddle ducks happen to be around. Then—and only then—if all is going well, it's time to move on to more difficult game.

Doves are one important example. A lot of dogs don't like fetching doves, and despite the appeal of starting the season with a fast and furious dove shoot, I usually leave the retrieving chores to one of the older dogs and wait until the youngster in the kennel has had a successful season under his belt before inviting him along. Doves have loose plumage and young dogs don't appreciate feathers sticking to their tongues. Equally important, dove hunting often takes place in very hot weather, and it's hard to pant holding a bird in your mouth. When I do take a young dog on his first dove hunt, I carry plenty of water in the vehicle, try to set up near a water source so the dog can cool down easily, and minimize the inevitable running around all enthusiastic dogs like to engage in, especially on the first hunt of the year. An overheated dog and a mouth full of dove feathers do not make a good combination, especially for a youngster.

The only reason sage hens aren't a problem for more retrievers is that not very many get to hunt them. Here in Montana, sage grouse and sharptail seasons open at the same time, but, as with doves, I prefer to leave young dogs behind on sage hen hunts until they've had a bit of experience. Probably because of a combination of the birds' size and pungency, dogs often balk the first time they encounter dead sage hens, and I prefer them to have mastered the basics on other species first.

Pheasants can cause problems for a young dog for very different reasons. In contrast to the species mentioned earlier, wounded pheasants like to run... and occasionally fight back. Running crip-

didn't make sense. A dead bird should have been an easy mark in the open creek bottom while a running cripple should have led the dog off into the brush. Scolding Sonny for his frivolous behavior, I slid down the bank to sort things out.

By the time I reached the water's edge, Sonny was tearing away at the bank like a pot-licker in search of a long forgotten bone. Composed of nothing but bare dirt and mud, the bank obviously couldn't hide a pheasant, so I called the dog off and set around the far side of the puddle to locate its route of escape. But when Sonny immediately returned to the bank, I paused to analyze the lie. Suddenly I realized that the undercut creek bank had collapsed, creating a potential space above the waterline. Just then the dog thrust his head below the water, scrabbled about beneath the bank, and emerged with one of the wiliest downed roosters it's ever been my privilege to collect. Nothing looks quite so bedraggled as a soaking wet pheasant, but the bird felt like a trophy as Sonny deposited it in my hand.

I read several morals into this simple story. If all apparent explanations for a missing bird seem impossible, look for another one. Dogs that can smell sometimes know more than people who can't. And above all, good dogs deserve the benefit of the doubt.

AND A PARTRIDGE IN A PEAR TREE

Like his contemporary Lester, Luke had his share of faults, and to be honest, he never was one of my favorite Labs. But he demonstrated a sweet disposition, had one of the gentlest mouths I've ever seen, and from time to time managed to embellish his generally plodding track record with something memorable.

One clear September afternoon, I deliberately left Sky back at

the kennel so I
Luke, his then
we started dow
to the floor of
coulee, he flus
tail that I dum
a rise over wh
of sight. Whe
crest, I could
had fallen int
dating sea of
Easterners
stuff take no

as devil's willow with good reason. There are
and thorns that stab, and buffalo berry falls s
ond category. As I listened to the dog work
brush below, I finally noticed a patch of gray
of the bushes like a Christmas tree ornamen
stone dead, the bird lay hung up in the thor
the ground and well out of the dog's reach..

I didn't relish the idea of wading through
climb the tree, but I wasn't raised to walk av
game either. Then as I studied the lay of th
plan my approach, I saw the tree begin to s
head appeared high above the ground, fran
foliage. After considerable commotion, dog
peared and a minute or so later Luke show
ing his prize.

I'm still not quite sure how he pulled c
know that his ingenuity and determinatic

erab
have

B show
out
colla
kenn
towa
clude
they

T
wasn'
the q
place
day. T
dent

Other People's Dogs

Can't we all just get along?

A s always, the opening day of Montana's bird season aroused the kind of fervor most of mankind reserves for religious holidays and World Cup soccer matches. Unable to sleep, I'd beaten the alarm by nearly an hour, leaving me with nothing to do but fiddle pointlessly with my gear and pace the floor until the rest of our hunting party arrived to pick me up. Sky only had one season under his belt then, but he seemed to know full well what was up, a realization he celebrated with an attack of eager whining and hysterical tail wagging as soon as I opened the kennel. Then we were off at last, headed east out of town toward a cool September sunrise and enough prairie bird cover to keep us occupied as long as four limits of sharptails would take.

We reached the ranch we planned to hunt right at first shooting light. Dividing into pairs, we set off along two long winding coulees to work the bushes for the first birds of the year. I happened to be hunting with a rather casual acquaintance handling a five year-old dog I will not identify by breed except to point out that it was not—repeat, not—a Lab. I really didn't know much about my companion and I knew even less about his dog, but so much great cover lay spread out before us that I couldn't imagine the skill level of either mattering much over the course of the morning.

Silly me. I will admit that my companion's dog possessed

strong legs and a capable nose. Unfortunately, that was the bad
news rather than the good. As soon as we started up the draw,
the dog tore off ahead in blissful defiance of the whistle blasts
that suddenly shattered the peace of what had so recently promised to be a gorgeous morning. When the dog reached the first
clump of brush, he attacked it like a wolf taking down an elk.
Yielding to this relentless assault, the bushes belched up a nice
covey of grouse, but since the rise took place two hundred yards
away there wasn't much we could do but watch as the birds
chuckled their way off into the pink eastern sky.

"Might want to work him a bit closer," I suggested diplomati-
cally.

"It's opening day," my companion replied cheerfully. "He'll
settle down."

But not, evidently, in my lifetime. For the next hour, I marked
the dog's course by the birds erupting in front of him while my
companion's whistle produced a shrill chorus that echoed relentlessly through the still morning air. The dog gave every appearance of being on the birds' payroll. Neither of us fired a shot.
Finally Sky set off in the direction of the party up ahead despite
my commands to the contrary, at which point I had to acknowledge that there was more at stake than an empty game vest.

"Think I'll head off and work the scrub around those bluffs," I
called across the draw as I pointed toward a distant line of cover.
I should have known better.

"Hang on and I'll catch up with you!" came the ringing reply.
To no great surprise; hunters who let their dogs run wild always
seem immune to the kind of hints that ordinarily grease the
wheels of social interactions. But by this time I'd had enough. In
the first place, it was opening day and I wanted to shoot some

birds. In the second, I was in danger of letting a promising youngster get sucked into a vortex of canine craziness. Feigning an acute attack of deafness, I set my legs into the hill and outran the competition, and Sky and I collected an easy limit in glorious solitude.

Fueled by morbid curiosity, I accepted an invitation to hunt with the same party later that month, just to see if the dog had settled down as promised. It hadn't. Over the course of another long morning, I offered a series of suggestions that ranged from the constructive (some concerted yard work with an e-collar) to the impolitic (euthanasia). Of course the latter proposal, delivered with deadpan conviction, effectively ended my hunting relationship with the dog's handler, but that was pretty much what I had in mind all along. All of which goes to show that loving a dog is pretty much like loving a spouse: blindness to fault can easily become an essential element of the relationship.

The idea is simply not to let it ruin everyone else's day.

I've never met a reasonable human being capable of resisting the charm of a retriever puppy. No doubt such people exist, but they are unlikely readers of this book, so the hell with them. But as dogs mature, they inevitably acquire traits that challenge the patience of their human companions. Dealing with those frustrating flaws in your own dog represents a technical challenge to your training ability. Dealing with difficult behavior in other people's dogs, however, remains a social issue capable of cementing or ruining friendships. Since friendships with people are almost as important as friendships with dogs, the subject deserves some consideration.

Worst-case scenarios like the one described earlier really leave just two options: endure or withdraw. The handler in question wasn't about to change anything or accept responsibility for his dog's behavior. In the name of friendship, I can put up with just about anything in the field except unethical hunting practices, unsafe gun handling, and conduct clearly deleterious to my own dogs. Cross one of those lines and it's time to vote with your feet and I did. No apologies needed, at least in my book.

Fortunately, hopeless situations prove the exception. Tactful suggestions to a friend can be both well received and constructive. I have certainly enjoyed the benefit of such advice over the years even if I found myself bridling a bit as I received it. That's a normal reaction; we tend to stick up for our dogs the same way we stick up for our kids. But learning how to take advice about your own dog also points the way to the correct way to offer it. Do unto others…no situation demonstrates the wisdom of the Golden Rule like dealing with misbehavior on the part of other people's dogs.

Someone once said that if you would know a man's character, you should share an inheritance with him. How about sharing a duck blind with someone else's young retriever? The combination of close quarters, canine enthusiasm, and nearby water can be enough to test any friendship, for good blind deportment is one of those traits easiest to appreciate in its absence. But mud and pond water wash off people and shotguns alike, and a bit of patience and good humor is usually all that's required to get through the morning. Of course, lots of ducks never hurt the cause.

While rambunctious behavior from a friend's dog can be inconvenient in a duck blind, upland work can test patience in different ways. Dogs are inherently more difficult to control at a distance, and the consequences of misbehavior usually result in more missed shooting opportunities in the field than in a blind.

But it's important to remember that all dogs need room to work, no matter who's handling them. It's always important to forgive occasional trespasses, just as you would expect your hunting partners to forgive when your dog trespasses against them.

Experienced handlers won't need to hear the cardinal rule in this situation but it's worth repeating anyway: No commands to other people's dogs! I would consider exceptions to this principle only if issues of safety were involved or if you have hunted with the other party long enough for both of you to feel comfortable with the practice, but that would have to be an awfully long time. Believe me.

Longstanding hunting relationships often breed a sense of friendly rivalry that extends to dog work as well as shooting, and that's fine as long as it doesn't get out of hand. Remember: it's one thing to boo my shooting but another matter entirely to boo my dog. Should you insist on doing so, remember the old advice from the cowboy movies and smile when you say that. And don't forget to cheer when your hunting partner's dog does something praiseworthy. Those two simple rules will go a long way toward preserving friendships in the field. Just remember how hard it is to find good hunting partners in the first place.

Since retriever enthusiasts tend to be so devoted to their own favorite breeds, the ribbing often grows particularly inspired when different dogs hunt together. For years, regular hunting partner Ray Stalmaster has handled Chessies, a situation that leads to all kinds of back and forth whenever our dogs are in the field at the same time. I admit enjoying an unfair advantage in these exchanges, since the most he could accuse my Labs of was sensitivity or lack of aggression while I had no end of material to criticize about his oily, bad-breathed, rock headed charges, but there you go. And yes, I was smiling when I said that.

Of course not all encounters with other people's dogs produce frustration. Dogs add to camaraderie in the field far more often than they detract. I've eaten a lot of birds flushed and retrieved by my friends' dogs and I've learned some valuable lessons watching other hunters work their dogs in the field. And for the most part I've enjoyed the company involved, human and otherwise.

In fact, hunting with an enthusiastic, well-trained dog that happens to belong to someone else can become a reliable pleasure, the kind you anticipate just as you look forward to the time you spend with your own dogs. After enough time in the field together, you get to know your friends' dogs and to regard them in a special way, just as you know and regard their children. And despite the trepidation first encounters with unfamiliar dogs can provoke, they can also provide some of the most enjoyable moments of all, especially if they come when you least expect them.

A few years back, a mutual friend introduced me to Bob May, proprietor of Whale Pass Lodge just north of Kodiak. I was bowhunting deer in the area at the time, but the invitation to shoot some ducks sounded like an offer I couldn't refuse. Yaeger, Bob's Chessie, impressed me as a likable dog as soon as I met him, but it was also obvious that Yaeger was a typical Alaska backcountry retriever, long on heart but short on formal training. I admit feeling a bit skeptical at first despite Bob's assurances. After all, have you ever met a Chessie owner who didn't think his dog was the greatest? But I also knew I wasn't going swimming in those frigid waters for downed ducks myself, so I accepted the offer of Yaeger's services with nothing more than my own silent reservations.

Yaeger spent the next five days showing me just how misplaced those reservations really were. The dog turned out to be an

absolute pleasure as he made one challenging retrieve after another look routine. If I hadn't already had a young Lab waiting for me to train back home, I would have accepted Bob's generous offer of a puppy in a heartbeat. When I returned home, I even made the mistake of admitting to Ray how impressed I'd been. He promptly hailed my new enlightenment as the first reasonable thing I'd said about retrievers in years. I didn't care; the dog had earned all the praise I gave him. And when I return to Kodiak as I do almost every year, I look forward to seeing Yaeger as much as any of my friends.

Maybe more. Sorry, Bob... nothing personal. That's just the way good dogs affect me.

Of course every time you set out with another hunter, the pride of your kennel becomes one of those other people's dogs in someone else's eyes. And as much as we might like to think otherwise, our own favorites are quite capable of producing embarrassing moments themselves. They all do it occasionally, even the best of them. When that happens, remember how it felt the last time the shoe was on the other foot and act accordingly. Don't become a co-dependent partner in the dog's misbehavior. Apologize as indicated (but no more). Offer your companion the opportunity to hunt in another direction. (He may decline on the assumption that a misbehaving dog is better than no dog, but that's his business). If you need to interrupt the hunt to work with the dog, by all means do so, but explain your intentions and give the rest of the party a chance to excuse themselves if they wish. When in doubt, do what you would expect others to do if their dogs were misbehaving. And remember always that your obligations to the dog are just as compelling as your obligations to your friends.

Other people's dogs have broken my heart and driven me to distraction and my dogs have done the same to others, sometimes in the same day. It pays to remember that a certain amount of unpredictability goes with the territory. If it were otherwise, the same dogs would win the same field trails every year at an incalculable savings of time and money. But how much fun would that be?

The margins of canine error may be broader in the field, but the basic balance sheet of triumph and disappointment remains pretty much the same. Whether the disappointment comes from your dog or your partner's, the guiding principle remains unchanged: be a gentleman about it, or a lady as the case may be. And who knows? The next time you hunt with someone else's dog, it might turn out to be another Yaeger.

My Kingdom for a Lab!

*Sometimes the best way to appreciate Labs
is by hunting without one*

The pungent smell of green mesquite filled our nostrils as we bounced down the road on our friend Ricardo's family ranch. As we passed a little two-acre tank, I noticed an assortment of ducks tucked up beneath the earthen dam. Ricardos' wife Josephina was due to join us at the hacienda for dinner that night, and we had just been discussing possibilities for the menu. "How about roast duck?" I asked.

"We can make an orange sauce!" Lori exclaimed, and that was all the motivation we needed to turn into impromptu duck hunters.

We had been bowhunting whitetails all week, and were hardly equipped for waterfowling in any classical sense of the word. However, Ricardo had two 20-gauge pumps back at the hacienda, and before long we were pulling an ouchy sneak through the thorn brush below the dam. While Ricardo insisted he wasn't much of a wing shot, his protests turned out to be false modesty. Neither of us missed a bird on the jump, and by the time the sound of the shooting faded away on the soft desert breeze a generous duck dinner lay scattered about the surface of the pond.

The scene would have provided a great opportunity for some enthusiastic dog work. Unfortunately, Jake and Sonny lay curled up in their kennels far away in Montana. "What are you going to do now?" Lori asked as she surveyed the glorious carnage.

There weren't a lot of choices. As ringleader of the escapade, I grit my teeth and stripped down to my skivvies. Warm mud oozed through my toes as I picked my way barefoot down to the waterline and tried to forget about all the snakes and snapping turtles we'd seen along the edges of the tanks earlier. "Fetch!" Lori cried helpfully from the shoreline, although I didn't find the circumstances nearly as humorous as she and Ricardo evidently did. Then I plunged in.

I won't pretend to have earned any marks for my water entry. Fortunately, every one of the birds lay stone dead, and the retrieves required neither speed nor olfactory acuity on my part. We had killed a splendid mixed bag of pintail, widgeon, and gadwall. An inexperienced waterfowler, Ricardo didn't know his ducks, and I pointed out their distinguishing field marks as I pitched them back toward shore, a service even the best canine retriever would be hard pressed to provide. Finally I fetched the last bird and we headed back to the hacienda for what eventually turned out to be a memorable course of wild duck grilled over mesquite coals. Unfortunately, before I could make an appearance in the kitchen to begin work on the meal, I had to spend the cocktail hour alone, soaking the mud and slime off my hide in a bathtub.

It just would have been so much easier with a Lab around…

For people like me who rise and retire every day in the company of retrievers, hunting birds without a dog sounds as farfetched as hunting birds without a shotgun. In fact, I would be hard pressed to remember the last time I killed a Montana game bird other than a turkey without a dog at my side.

Granted, sometimes those dogs were too young to serve with flair and sometimes they belonged to someone else, but they were always there, as essential to the hunting experience as a valid license.

But circumstances sometimes conspire successfully against even the most devoted retriever enthusiast, often as the result of travel. Transporting dogs through the airline system can be stressful to dog and handler alike, and unless I'm going on a trip primarily focused on wingshooting, I'm usually reluctant to accept that kind of hassle. But because I travel a lot on fly-fishing and bowhunting assignments, I wind up in wild places full of game birds without a dog a lot more often than I'd like. Even in unfamiliar circumstances, a dedicated hunter can usually beg, borrow or steal a shotgun and enough shells to sample the local shooting. Serviceable dogs, as we all know well, invariably prove a lot harder to come by.

Diverse agendas also cause problems. As much as I love my Labs and my shotguns, I spend a lot of time in the field pursuing other interests, and retrievers aren't always the best company when stalking elk or spring creek brown trout. And hard as it might be for us to imagine, our companions on these non-wing-shooting ventures have the right to bridle at the thought of a dog in camp. Of course, most of my own friends have grown accustomed to the idea of sharing space with wet Labs in tents, drift boats, and bush planes, but I'd still be reluctant to ask that kind of tolerance from anyone I didn't know well.

Nothing can make you appreciate absent dogs like the pursuit of waterfowl. Flushing retrievers have become so popular among upland hunters that it's easy for many of us to forget that these breeds all evolved as water dogs. Nothing enforces that history lesson quite like a dead duck in a frigid pond when your favorite canine companion is somewhere else. Of course, lack of a serviceable dog often precludes waterfowling entirely, and in many circumstances the only responsible course of action is to leave the shotgun in its case. Nonetheless, I occasionally talk myself into hunting ducks without a dog, fully aware how quickly these ventures can cross the arbitrary line between enthusiasm and folly.

A few Novembers ago, I traveled north to Kodiak Island to meet my old friends Doug Borland and Ernie Holland, both Alaska residents. Doug had drawn a Kodiak bear tag and he meant to kill the bear with his longbow or not at all. The primary mission for Ernie and me was to take turns backing Doug up with the .375 in case his bear hunt turned ugly, always a possibility when confronting thousand pound brown bears with stick and string. On our days off, we stalked Sitka blacktail deer with our own bows and hunted ducks along the mouth of the saltwater lagoon where we had camped. Without a dog, we had to retrieve our downed birds with the tiny inflatable boat we had brought along to cross the outlet of the lagoon. You didn't have to be an experienced mariner to recognize the craft as scarcely adequate for the purpose.

The first afternoon I set out with the shotgun, I set up inside the mouth of the lagoon and promptly dropped a drake Barrow's goldeneye that made the mistake of taking a shortcut across the spit. The tide was running, and it was all I could do to paddle fast enough to catch up to the dead bird. I had promised everyone a duck dinner, and by the time I collected enough birds for the dish I had in mind, I'd decided I was through using a glorified bathtub toy to do a job that rightfully belonged to a Labrador retriever.

The following morning, we all rose in the dark and set out across the mouth of the lagoon in the little boat so we could head up the mountain before daylight. Halfway across, I heard an ominous hiss bearing down upon us in the current. The tide had lifted loose a sheet of ice at the head of the bay, and before we could take evasive action its sharp leading edge had sliced through the boat like a knife through butter, depositing us unceremoniously in the north Pacific. We were only forty yards from shore, but with heavy hunting boots and a full pack on my back that turned into one of the longest swims of my life. The air temperature stood well below freezing, and by the time we staggered back to camp and lit a fire we were all as close to the Big Chill as we'd been in some time. "Just think," I finally managed to observe. "During duck season, the dogs do that twenty times a day!" Needless to say, that was the end of the duck hunting on that trip.

Because retrievers are bred to withstand water far better than people, ducks and geese usually provide the keenest appreciation of their absence. However, upland game provides its own share of opportunities to offer one's kingdom for an experienced retriever. The dogs themselves bear some responsibility for our own shortcomings when it comes time to locate a downed pheasant or grouse. Those who learn to hunt birds without dogs subconsciously develop marking skills right from the start as a matter of necessity. On the other hand, people like me who grew up with good dogs beside us in the field often lack that unpracticed ability. I admit that I tend to look reflexively for the back half of a double when I should be paying attention to the location of a fall, a luxury decades of competent dog work has allowed me to take for granted.

Whatever one's skill level recovering game unassisted, some birds are certain to exceed it and they are no doubt better left alone, at least until another day. I simply refuse to hunt pheasants

without a retriever, without exception. Hunting wild ringnecks
without a capable dog amounts to little more than feeding coyotes, an outcome I respect the quarry too much to accept.
Fortunately, almost all my pheasant hunting takes place within
fifty miles of my house, so as long as I remember to take one of
the dogs along no matter what the trip's primary mission, I seldom have to test my own restraint.

Most of my own retrieving takes place when I've packed a
shotgun along on a bowhunting trip, and it doesn't always go
badly. Ptarmigan, for example, have fed me on countless caribou
and sheep hunts. Despite their protective coloration, ptarmigan
generally inhabit open ground and lack the ringneck's tenacious
instincts for escape, making it possible to recover the vast majority of downed birds even without a dog. Good thing; after a long
day spent hiking across the tundra, grilled ptarmigan breasts can
be a welcome addition to any camp menu.

Desert quail are another matter. Retrievers may not be classic
quail dogs, but I've never missed mine more than while hunting
Gamble's and blues incidental to the pursuit of big game in
Arizona, Texas, and Mexico. Quail offer more chances for snappy
doubles than any game bird I know, but when you're hunting
without a capable retriever you might as well forget about your
second barrel. And while desert bird cover may not require much
swimming, its flora all boast intimidating thorns and downed
quail have a nasty habit of falling into the worst. I don't know
how the dogs manage to pick their way through the stuff, but
they clearly know something I don't. A retriever makes such a
huge difference on desert quail that I usually take one of the dogs
along when I venture into quail country nowadays, even when the
prime purpose of the trip has nothing to do with wingshooting.

The inconvenience of transporting dogs on domestic airline flights pales in comparison to the difficulties of international travel, which is why I've never enjoyed an opportunity to hunt with one of my own Labs in Africa. That isn't all bad. One afternoon I dropped a pair of turtledoves into a pool of stagnant water near the Save River in southern Zimbabwe. As I tried to decide how to retrieve them, I noticed a large crocodile's unmistakable skid mark leading from the opposite bank into the pool. I wound up teasing the floating doves into shore with the aid of a long stick that didn't feel nearly long enough. I hated to think of what might have happened had one of the dogs been with me. The thought of Sonny disappearing in a swirl like a surface popper struck by a hungry pike proved so unsettling that I finally abandoned the water hole despite the clouds of doves overhead.

But I also remember times in Africa when I would have given anything for one of the dogs. One night in the Namibian desert, I set my bow aside and picked up my .410 double at sundown. Ten minutes later, the sand grouse arrived right on schedule, silhouetted against the glow in the western sky as their haunting liquid cries filled the air. The shooting only lasted a few minutes, but a dozen birds lay scattered about the water hole by the time I quit. I had to retrieve them by flashlight, a process that seemed to take forever as the sounds of the veldt rose from the darkness. By the time I heard the first lion cough, the .410 felt smaller than it ever had before and the absence of a dog to help finish the job seemed as huge as the night itself.

The mallards came spiraling down out of the winter sky as if by magic, and when I rose to take them two plump drakes hit the water as the rest of the flock clawed its way toward safety.

Jake hit the creek in a cloud of spray, returning the first bird to my hand before the second could drift beyond the lower reaches of the pool where the decoys lay bobbing in the current. By the time he brought me the second duck, I had already broken down my gun and waded into the water to begin picking up the blocks. Remarkable, I thought to myself as I accepted the last bird and tossed it into the pile behind me on the bank. And it was.

The remarkable thing about the morning's hunt, of course, was how absolutely unremarkable collecting that limit had been. I didn't have to think about anything other than the shooting. The dog had taken care of everything that followed, with nothing but a minimum of guidance from me. There have been days when I wouldn't have given his performance a second thought, but this wasn't one of them. I'd traveled a lot that fall, and I still remembered what it was like to shoot without a dog at my side.

Jake sat patiently on the bank while I finished collecting the decoys. Back at the truck, I let him hop into the cab next to the heater. He had earned a warm ride home. Whatever his faults, and he has his share too, they paled before the thought of hunting without him. Absence had truly made the heart grow fonder.

Perhaps he wondered why I gave his ears an extra scratch as we started for home, although I suspect he knew all along.

Requiem for a Middleweight

*In the measure of dogs' lives, only those who have
known them can set the rules*

The roosters came boiling up out of the brush in a sudden
explosion of noise and color, wings straining toward the
possibility of escape, long tails silhouetted against the azure
autumn sky. The dog had done the hard part. All I had to do was
kill two to go with the single I'd collected earlier and I did, and
the shooting would have been as routine as two steps forward to
the station on a skeet range if it hadn't been for the long push
through the thorns that earned us the rise in the first place.
When the back half of the lazy double tumbled into the willows,
I broke the gun, pocketed the empties, and waited for Sonny to
clean up what was left so we could head for home and the dinner
Lori and I had promised another couple that night.

But Sonny had other ideas. The breeze hadn't even dispersed
the smell of the powder by the time he delivered the first bird,
but at that point he suddenly staged a rebellion. Correctly no
doubt, he sensed the presence of more birds ahead of us in the
cover, and since the state of Montana's idea of enough pheasants
for one day didn't agree with his own, he decided to ignore the
second fall and keep hunting. Blasting peevishly on the whistle, I
finally retrieved the retriever, reinforced the line, and sent him on
his way. Like a missile with a scrambled guidance system, he tore
off down the creek bank on a perpendicular vector, and it took

me ten minutes to call him back to my side. By the time we finally collected the missing bird, the sun had retreated behind the skyline to the west and my plans for a leisurely hour in the kitchen before our guests' arrival had sunk right along with it.

That's the kind of delightfully addled performance you'd expect in the field from a promising dog in his derby year, but Sonny happened to be nine at the time, with more wild birds under his belt than most dogs would enjoy in several lifetimes. And I'll admit that as I set my legs against the hillside for the long walk back through the gloom toward the truck, the relationship between dog and hunter felt noticeably strained. But then common sense prevailed. The evening air felt cool and refreshing. Miles from the nearest telephone, I had a limit of pheasants resting in my game vest. And our friends could wait a few extra minutes for dinner; if they couldn't they wouldn't be our friends.

This was a bird hunt, not a field trial, and if Sonny could forgive me a miss from time to time, I should be able to forgive him an occasional lack of discipline. I knew he'd do the same for me.

Hunting dog enthusiasts enjoy abundant opportunities to read stories about dogs whose championship performances inspire us all and define the standards of our favorite breeds. This will not be one of them.

Years ago when I lived in Alaska and spent more time than I care to remember landing airplanes in ridiculous places, I read a lengthy critique of a particular model of bush plane whose manufacturer I will not embarrass in print. The reviewer, an old time bush pilot who had logged thousands of tough hours in the aircraft, began by describing a list of faults that went on for pages. His terse conclusion read: Best damn airplane I ever flew.

For most retriever enthusiasts who operate outside the ordered world of field trials and their relatively objective measures of canine ability, a summary of our own favorite dogs' liabilities and assets might run along similar lines. Because of the attachment we form with our dogs after years together in the field, we tend to cut straight to the bottom line, and why not? We all know a best damn dog I ever owned. But faults remain—no doubt more apparent to our hunting partners than to ourselves—and pretending they don't exist does a certain injustice both to the dogs and those who hunt with them.

In fact, Sonny—or West Wind's Sunrise, to use the formal address appropriate to an old soldier at the end of his career—is not the best damn dog I ever owned, although on his good days he could make a compelling argument to the contrary. And like the beat-up old bush plane referenced earlier, a list of his shortcomings would run to page length. Highlights? Why not; this chapter is born in the spirit of candor. Nose: good but not great. Marking ability: likewise. Handling: fair. Tractability: headstrong to a fault. Athleticism: marginal, at least in water. Appearance: about as attractive as his owner. Poor guy.

While none of this sounds like much of an advertisement, Sonny was one of the most enjoyable dogs to hunt with (or be around) I've ever known. While that endorsement sounds a bit like being named Best Personality at a beauty contest, it's not the biased product of my own affection. Virtually everyone I know who spent any time with him felt pretty much the same way. And therein lies this essay's thesis: working retrievers earn their way into our hearts by means that defy easy explanation. No test can readily define those qualities, and even words—no matter how carefully labored over—usually come up short in the end. But words are my job, so bear with me while I try.

Before striving for intangibles, I feel I owe it to Sonny to balance the ledger of his faults in the field, abundant as they may have been. He always demonstrated a wonderful mouth, and the many birds he brought to hand inevitably arrived at the table in impeccable condition. Although not the strongest swimmer I've ever hunted with, he proved tenacious in upland cover and made a career of tireless days in rugged western terrain. While he never marked with pinpoint accuracy, he would work the area of a fall as if it owed him money, and never quit unless I asked him to. But while these are all desirable traits that would be readily apparent to any knowledgeable hunter, they fall far short of defining the dog.

When the Labrador retriever's ancestors crawled out of the cold north Atlantic centuries ago, they defined a job description that remained unchanged until relatively recently. Labs fetched ducks, and for years all the breed's formal standards reflected that imperative. Nowadays, working Labs probably spend as much

time in upland cover as they do in duck blinds, but standards for a flushing Lab's role in the field remain difficult to articulate, let alone teach. Doing it right remains a gift, and Sonny had it.

No upland quarry demands more of flushing retrievers than pheasants, and Sonny understood pheasants the same intuitive way musicians understand their instruments. I'd like to be able to pretend I taught him all the pheasant hunting tricks he mastered, but that would be wishful thinking. All I really did was give him plenty of opportunity, since I live where the birds are and have structured my life shamelessly around their pursuit, but opportunity was largely the extent of my own contribution. I've given other dogs the same kind of exposure to wild birds, but none profited from their time afield quite the same way. Sonny took pheasant hunting personally and it showed.

While ringnecks brought out his best, Sonny hardly spent his career as a one-dimensional hunter. I've trained a number of dogs that could out-perform him in the water, but Sonny proved himself the master of one under-appreciated element of life in the duck blind: waiting. Some of the best waterdogs I've ever worked with quickly become tedious company whenever the action slows, but Sonny's relentless patience in the face of empty skies often inspired me keep hunting far longer than I might have on my own. Together, we enjoyed more late morning limits than I can count. Bowhunting has taught me more about the virtues of patience than most waterfowlers will ever know, but long hours in the field still go best in the company of a friend. In the duck blind, I've never known a better one.

Like art itself, enthusiasm in a hunting dog remains an elusive quantity, difficult to define in its absence but impossible not to appreciate when it's staring you in the face. If I had to identify one character trait that compensated for all Sonny's technical shortcomings, my search would begin and end with that single word. Any good dog can show its heart when there's a duck kicking in the decoys or fresh scent leading off through the brambles, but Sonny elevated canine enthusiasm to remarkable levels of anticipation. Even if we weren't going hunting, he read the possibility into all the activities of daily life around the house, wagging his tail if I happened past the gun cabinet and making eager feints toward the truck whenever I paused before the rack of hunting clothes in the mud room. That kind of attitude proves contagious, and while I'll never know how many extra birds his enthusiasm produced over the years, it certainly provided me with plenty of motivation. As if I needed it.

Reviewing these notes, I realize that they sound an awful lot like an obituary. Not true, thank goodness; in fact, this chapter's subject lies farting happily beneath my desk as I write. But at the end of last season, Sonny and I experienced a qualitative change in our relationship. One cold, blustery day I dropped a mallard into the decoys for what should have been a routine retrieve. Sonny walked down to the waterline, stared briefly at the bird, walked back to the blind, and curled up at my feet. That was it; he was twelve years old and he didn't want to do it anymore. I didn't bother to ask him twice. When a dog like Sonny announces his retirement, you don't question the decision.

In a way, I felt grateful. I've known good old Labs who just wouldn't quit, leaving their handlers the untenable choice of refusing to allow their dogs to do what they love or watching them endure hunting conditions beyond their capacity. Like a veteran boxer who knows just when to walk away from the ring and all its glory, Sonny called an end to his career with impeccable timing. There's no skill in all sport as difficult as going out a winner, as I'll probably have to remind myself one day. Leave it to an old dog to show how to do it right.

While this new state of affairs has yet to stand the test of an opening day, I'm pleased to report that so far Sonny has accepted his retirement with uncommon grace. I learned years ago that

most of my friends like my parents, my kids, my wife and my dogs more than they like me, a judgement so reasonable it's never occurred to me to resent it. When fellow hunters stop by the house, it never takes them long to seek out Sonny, and he inevitably receives their good will with the kind of knowing affection guaranteed to set off rounds of reminiscence about seasons past when he was younger as, for that matter, were we. As a writer, I receive lots of calls and letters from Lab enthusiasts around the country and I'm always amazed to note how many of them ask about Sonny as if he were an old friend. My God, I sometimes think to myself. Has the old rascal really demanded that much of my attention in print? Evidently.

But what about that long compendium of faults outlined earlier? In the end, I think they're precisely the point. To paraphrase Shakespeare: To err is canine...Most of us will never hunt with a field trial champion, let alone go through the long, arduous process of training one. Leave it to those rare princes to set the standards while the rest of us kiss our share of toads. The final compliment to the retrievers that enrich our lives may stem from the capacity of each and every one to offer us something unique and irreplaceable.

We can only hope our friends will someday feel the same about us.

A Dog for All Seasons

The Lab's greatest accomplishment: being so
many things to so many people

The air that morning felt cold enough to bite. As the current tumbled past the fallen cottonwood, steam rose from the water and coated the brush along the banks in layers of rime. And when the sun finally cleared the eastern horizon, Sky looked dressed up to match our surroundings, with a layer of sparkling frost framing his muzzle in the clear morning light. If he felt cold he was too proud to show it, and as I stomped out a nest in the snow and settled back against the log, he turned his attention upward and began to scan the air overhead for ducks. You can't teach a dog that kind of enthusiasm, but when you're hunting with a good one you don't have to.

We didn't have to wait long. The sound of whistling wings soon rose from the darkest corner of the sky and by the time we saw the mallards approaching the birds already had their flaps down and their landing gear extended. The shooting itself was kid stuff, and by the time the ejectors spat the empties into my gloved hand one drake lay stone dead across the creek while a second bobbed gently away on the current.

I whistled Sky off the easy mark and gave him a line on the floating bird. Sky had been at this long enough to trust me. He hit the water in a geyser of spray and zeroed in on the floater like a heat-seeking missile. Although frowned upon in proper circles, I let my dogs run the banks when we're hunting creeks and rivers simply because I want them out of the current and back at my side as soon as possible. When Sky burst from the brush with the bird in his mouth—delivered in its usual impeccable condition—I accepted the delivery and sent him for the second duck. And within minutes of the first flock's arrival, we were back in place waiting for the second, an exercise in efficiency that paid off when a single dropped in from behind us only to wind up added to the little pile resting on the cottonwood log.

What remains remarkable about this brief canine performance turned in years ago by a dog no longer with us? Nothing and everything, according to the perspective of the observer—which happens to be precisely the point. Now that the Labrador retriever is officially the most popular dog breed in America, it should come as no surprise that different Lab owners entertain wildly varying expectations for their charges. And a few minutes one dog spent retrieving a pair of ducks on a brisk winter morning could mean different things to any of them.

Even after three decades of living with Labs and hunting them as much as seasons and circumstances allow, I remain an outsider to a certain hard core of the retriever contingent simply because I don't field trial my dogs. While I remain sufficiently devoted to the breed to regard this attitude defensively, I grant my critics a point. Field trials define standards for the working retriever that remain hard to argue, and whether they realize it or not, all Lab enthusiasts owe the field trial process an incalculable measure of gratitude. A century of such tradition—only occasionally acknowledged to the extent it deserves—is all that stands between the dogs we know and mutts.

But no system of standards remains infallible and those of us who hunt with Labs should reserve the right to break the rules as we see fit. Running a bank may represent a serious fault in field trial circles. But when I've sent one of my own into flowing water after a late season mallard I want the dog back on dry land as soon as possible, for a variety of reasons ranging from more efficient duck hunting to canine safety. If orthodoxy must be challenged to achieve this result, so be it. I'll trade adherence to someone else's ideals for a limit of ducks and a happy dog any day, because those are the standards I've set for my Labs under the conditions we face together in the field.

Here in the out-of-the-way west—an area removed both geographically and culturally from the heart of the field trial tradition—snubbing authority remains a way of life whether the rules in question represent standards for hunting dogs or dictates of government. Nonetheless, I'm not offering an anti-field trial screed. But I do acknowledge the ability of hunting Labs to improvise, and the obligation of their handlers to accommodate them.

While some might cite lack of discipline in their critique of Sky's performance that morning, others—perhaps a majority in this day and age of the Lab's extended appeal—might complain about its excess. The thermometer hovered just above zero. Conditions were miserable before I issued the command to fetch and sent him plunging into the water. How could anyone who cares about Labs have asked one to make such a retrieve? To which I would respond: How could I have refused to?

Those who do not learn from history are condemned to repeat it, and in this vein I would suggest that no one who owns a Lab can understand their charge without an appreciation of the breed's origins. The Labs we know today evolved—and I choose this verb deliberately, in the Darwinian sense—from British stock imported to assist early Devonshire emigrants who fished the coast of Newfoundland centuries ago. The North Atlantic remains an unforgiving place today; back then, those who could not adapt—human, canine or otherwise—simply disappeared one way or another. Labs meant to survive fetched buoys and nets and climbed back aboard fishing boats by hauling their way up lines with their teeth. Those that failed to master these skills spent their DNA elsewhere. A modern Lab hitting frigid water with a splash isn't avoiding punishment but fulfilling its destiny.

Asked to summarize the Lab's distinctive personality in one word, I'd reply: enthusiasm. And one of the breed's most remarkable traits remains its ability to demonstrate enthusiasm towards almost anything: dead birds, a walk in the park, the toddler pulling at the dog's ears. But finding ways to love whatever's happening still differs from doing what one is born to do. Jumping into a river on a cold winter day may not be our idea of a good time, but Labs see things differently. Non-hunting Lab lovers willing to keep an open mind really should try to find a way to invite themselves along on some of these adventures. A morning or two in a duck blind with the right dog is still the best way to understand the essential character of the Labrador retriever.

Given the increasingly broad base of the breed's popularity, the appearance of more and more Labs in non-hunting households becomes inevitable. Many such members of this new generation of Lab enthusiasts demonstrate attitudes toward hunting that range from unfulfilled interest to indifference to (in some unfortunate circumstances) downright antagonism. As with politics, religion, and similar issues of impassioned principle, tolerance for opposing views has a lot to be said for it, and who knows? Perhaps love of Labs will provide a badly needed catalyst for reconciliation between hunting, non-hunting, and even anti-hunting outdoor enthusiasts. It's certainly hard to imagine a better-qualified ambassador of goodwill than an enthusiastic Labrador retriever.

While I'm all for patience and understanding among Lab owners with different interests, a few caveats remain. In the years ahead, more and more Lab litters will be bred to satisfy the interests of owners removed from the breed's original hunting traditions. The fact that Labs make great house pets doesn't mean the breed should be reduced to its lowest common denominator. One tampers with success at one's own risk. To a greater extent than any other hunting dog, the Lab has found ways to satisfy the needs of non-hunting owners. That may be the breed's greatest accomplishment, but it might also be its eventual undoing. Remarkably, this transition has come to pass without compromising the Lab's ability to perform in the field... so far. We all owe it to these remarkable animals to keep their sudden popularity from altering future generations beyond recognition.

Another Lab, another season. Dry grass crunches underfoot and the whole prairie feels as if it's sizzling beneath the Indian summer sun. Cold water and late season duck hunts seem as far removed as the Lab's original stomping grounds on the shores of the North Atlantic. No matter; Sonny's never met a hunting trip he didn't like.

How the dog can smell anything under such miserable scenting conditions remains beyond me, but we've both learned a trick or two about September sharptail hunting over the years. The first is to save the dog from his own nearly hysterical early season enthusiasm, which is why he's plodding along at heel against his wishes. The second is to remember Sutton's Law and concentrate our efforts where the money is. That's why we're heading for the buffalo berry bushes.

The first dense clump of brush offers the only shade we've seen since we left the truck. Flushing birds single-handed from its depths would be an exercise in futility. Even if I could fight my way through the thorns to reach them, I'd never be able to get a shot off from the middle of that spiny jungle. That's where the dog comes in, and Sonny knows it.

Positioning myself on the rise overlooking the brush, I cluck softly to the dog and the long off-season's worth of tedium comes to a glorious end as Sonny bounds down the hill and launches into the cover. Moments later, the first bird of the year erupts into the azure sky and crumples at the shotgun's report—the second one, I must admit. Finally, it's time for the dog to do what he's been bred to: retrieve.

As Sonny charges back up the hill with the bird in his mouth, I pause to consider the wonderfully variable job description the breed commands today, from field trial champions to civilian pot-lickers. Because I live in good hunting country that offers a long menu of outdoor experiences, I sometimes think I've exposed my dogs to all the variety they could ask for, but I've really just scratched the surface. From the pressures of the field trial circuit to laid back evenings in front to the fireplace with the kids, Labs have found ways to do it all, without changing their essential character.

We owe it to the dogs to keep it that way.